'WE SURVIVED'

Collected Memories of School Days
at PLC Armidale - 1936 to 1964

Edited by
Christine Perrott

Copyright © Christine Perrott, 2021
Published: 2021 by The Book Reality Experience

ISBN: 978-0-6451532-7-9 - Paperback Edition

ISBN: 978-0-6451532-9-3 - EBook Edition

All rights reserved.

The right of Christine Perrott to be identified as the author of this Work has been asserted by her in accordance with sections 77 and 78 of the Copyright, Designs and Patents Act 1988.

This book is a memoir, reflecting the contributors' present recollections of experiences over time. This means that some details may vary from fact. Some names and characteristics may have been changed, some events may have been compressed, and some dialogue may have been recreated. Memory can be a fickle thing, so the editor trusts that any minor errors in times, dates and details of particular events will be understood.

All imagery is used with permission of the accredited source and copyright of individual images remains with the original provider. No image may be used without approval by the accredited source. All enquiries are to be made to the publisher in the first instance. All rights are reserved.

No part of this publication may be reproduced, stored in a retrieval system, copied in any form or by any means, electronic, mechanical, photocopying, recording or otherwise transmitted without written permission from the publisher.

Cover Design by Luke Buxton | www.lukebuxton.com
Cover photo: Main House (*Birida*) with the classroom block in the background and Armidale PLC girls in the grounds, 1956. Courtesy PLC Archives.

For my PLC Armidale teachers,
Gwen Kelly, History
and
Joyce Adams, Music
who gave me skills and knowledge resulting in
life-long pleasure and enjoyment

Table of Contents

Prologue i
PART ONE
  The War and Immediate Post-War Years
    Introduction 1
    Dorothy McRae (née Curtis) 1936-1946 3
    Betty Joyce (née Harden) mid 1930s-1945 6
    Nancye Rew (née Pullen) 1942-1946 7
    Barbara Brett 1944-1948 11
    Peggy Craddock (née Wilkinson) 1945-1949 13
    Rosemary Perrott-Russell (née Perrott) 1949-1954 16
    Pam Harvey (née Davidson) 1947-1951 17
    Janice Holcombe (née Todd) 1947-55 18
    Laurel McCosker (née Cole) 1945-1947 19
    Maureen Smith 1948-50s 20
    Jean Ferguson (née Muir) 1946-1954 20
    Images Set A 23
PART TWO
  The Early 1950s
    Introduction 33
    Dinah Roepers (née Burnett) 1952-1953 34
    Gweneth Berman (née McKenzie) 1949-1951 37
    Gerlinde Spencer (née Braunschweig) 1951-52 38
    Toni Playford (née Yates) 1953-1955 51
    Beth McKee tells of her sister's experience in 1953 55
    Barbara McHattan (née Reid) 1950-1958 55
    Annabelle Sinclair 1949-1956 56

Heather Bardsley (née Briggs Davie) 1953-1955 58
Heather Benning (née Noon) 1950-1958 59
Margaret Davidson (née Brett) 1949-1953 60
Janet Witham (née Weatherburn) 1954-1956 62
Beth McKee (née Clyne) 1954-1958 67
Patricia Harrison 1950-1956 67
Images Set B 75

PART THREE

The Late 1950s and Early 1960s

Introduction 85
Christine Prowse (née Heydon) 1957-1963 87
Jenny Johnson (née Burnett) 1955-1956 93
Margaret Nowak (née Willis) 1954-1955 95
Pamela Pike (née Golland) 1956-1958 99
Catherine Gough (née McKechnie) 1954-57 100
Lorna Lewis (née Pitkin) 1953-1957 103
Christine Perrott (née Ewing) 1953-1957 107
Sally Cater (née Mills) 1948-1959 113
Jill Longworth (née Eames) 1956-1957 115
Jo Hawthorne (née McArthur) 1960-64 122
Sally Robertson (née Price) 1961-1964 123
Marlene Pearce (née Dew) 1960-1963 126
Images Set C 127

Epilogue 137
Headmistresses of Hilton & PLC Armidale 1909-1968 139
Acknowledgements 140
About the Editor 141
Publisher's Comment 143

Prologue

The genesis of this book occurred in the conversations at the inaugural Birida Bunch reunion held in 2018 for Presbyterian Ladies College (PLC) Old Girls from the era when the school was sited on a large suburban block within the city of Armidale. Its frontage was Brown Street and on the eastern and western sides respectively ran Marsh and Faulkner Streets. Those attending the brunch had attended PLC Armidale sometime during the period from 1936 to 1962 when it was at the 110 Brown Street address.

They were affectionately being called The Birida Bunch because the original residence on the Brown Street site, known as Main House to the boarders, was called *Birida*.

The exchange of stories between these Old Girls revealed a boarding school life quite different to that experienced today. The school's enrolment numbers hovered around 100 and, in three boarding houses, Prep House, Junior House and Main House and a separate classroom block, the girls followed a set daily routine. The reminisces about this routine shared at the brunch were hilarious, shocking, amazing, sometimes unbelievable, fascinating, extraordinary and passionate. They were speaking about times which constitute an important part of our social history and should not be forgotten.

Thus it was decided to collect reminisces from Armidale PLC Old Girls of this era and create an entertaining and informative book about boarding school life from just before World War II until the early 1960s.

PLC Armidale is one of the few pre-Kindergarten to Year 12 all-girls day and boarding schools in regional NSW. It developed from the days in the late 19th century when Armidale was seen as a mecca of education, healthy climate and religious observance. *Hilton Girls School* was one of the early schools in Armidale and Armidale Presbyterian School Pty Ltd bought this school from its Headmistress, Miss Alethea Tendall in 1938, creating the first girls school in northern NSW linked to the Presbyterian Church.

The large block fronting Brown Street which became PLC Armidale's campus was originally privately owned and is graced with a Federation residence, *Birida*. It was purchased in 1940 by Armidale Presbyterian School Pty Ltd.

Armidale Presbyterian School Pty Ltd went into voluntary liquidation in 1940, transferred its assets to the Presbyterian Church and the school became PLC Armidale with the name *Hilton PLC*.

There was sufficient land at the *Birida* block for the building of a two storied classroom block with toilet facilities, extra wide staircase, five upstairs classrooms, a library and staff room and two downstairs classrooms, an assembly room and the Headmistress's office.

Later a dining hall building was erected and there was space in the grounds for basketball (netball) and tennis courts and a large enough yard area to play team softball and carry out group recreational pursuits sitting on picnic rugs.

A large building with a loft, in the past used by the *Birida* household as a stables and for horse feed storage, became an art space (the loft), a gym (a large ground floor room with a small dais or stage at one end) and a series of smaller rooms for science, music and sewing classes. Some nearby cottages became included in the campus and were used as boarding houses, a staff residence and a hospital with a live-in Sister.

There was always planning for growth and in relation to this, the Presbyterian Church purchased a large block of land on the north hill of Armidale. This became euphemistically known as 'The Promised Land'.

The first Speech Day at The Promised Land site was held in 1960 and a gradual rehousing of the school took place thereafter. A formal opening celebration was held on 17 September,1964. The upgraded facilities were a marked improvement on those at the *Birida* campus.

Thus, the *Birida* era ranged from early 1940s to early 1960s, was the beginning of the school as PLC and the choice of many families for the education of their daughters.

PART ONE

The War and Immediate Post-War Years

Introduction

Although Armidale had a reputation for being a city of churches and schools it was, in the first half of the 20th century, still a relatively small regional city in country New South Wales.

In 1941 Hilton Presbyterian Girls School was renamed Hilton PLC Armidale. War worries abounded and, like many towns and cities, Armidale built air raid shelters some in the form of trenches around the Armidale Teachers College (ATC). ATC also stored in their basement some treasures evacuated for safety from the Public Library of Sydney.

Armidale was spared war traumas unlike Darwin, some coastal towns in WA, Newcastle and Sydney with the mini Japanese submarines in their harbour. However, a Prisoner of War Control Centre was set up in Jessie Street and about 40 Italian POWs were dispersed to rural properties to replace the labour loss from young men joining our armed forces. In 1943 rationing of some items began.

In 1944 the Intermediate Certificate, undertaken in the third year of secondary school, became assessed partly by the school and partly by external exams.

War hostilities stopped in Europe in May 1945 and in September victory was achieved in the Pacific (VP). All over Australia, including Armidale, festivities and victory marches occurred celebrating VP. PLC girls joined the town march along Beardy Street.

The Sydney Symphony Orchestra became a full time body under the auspices of the ABC in 1946 and gradually developed a regular regional tour which included Armidale. These concerts were a highlight for PLC girls.

East West Airways began flights between Armidale and Sydney in 1947 but a DC3 crash near Quirindi the following year drew attention to air travel's dangers. Also in 1948 the first Holden rolled off the assembly line. This same year the death occurred of Howard Hinton, donor of many art works to ATC, now held at New England Regional Art Museum, Kentucky Street (NERAM).

In 1949 a polio epidemic swept through Australia and Armidale did not escape. PLC girls had to be inoculated and one contracted this vicious disease. This year also saw The Armidale School (TAS) taken over by the Anglican Diocese of Armidale and the external exams for the Intermediate Certificate abandoned. Australia seemed to be growing up, with voting rights given to Aborigines and the start of the construction of the Snowy Hydro Scheme.

Dorothy McRae (née Curtis) 1936-1946

I am an **OLD** Old Girl having commenced at Hilton when it was on the corner of Dangar and Brown Streets, Armidale. It was called Hilton, then for a short time Hilton PLC and then just PLC. I was only ever a day girl and can't remember even peeping into the Boarding House.

I first was a pupil in Miss Cooper's kindergarten where so many of my friends went in that era. Her kindergarten was on the corner of Mann Street and Jessie Street. In 1935 I left Miss Cooper's and went to Hilton. The Headmistress was Miss Tendall, followed by Dr Wilkie and then Miss Ashworth. I can't remember a single unhappy day; I loved everything.

One event I remember so very clearly. I was called out of class and told I was wanted on the phone. I was taken to an office room and it had a telephone on the wall. I remember this because I had trouble reaching it. The call was from Kiola Private Hospital telling me that I had a baby brother. I can remember vividly saying, 'Daddy will be so happy and so surprised. I can't wait to run down to the shop after school and tell him'. This was in 1937 when my brother Robert was born. I had no idea my mother was pregnant, a baby was never mentioned and I never saw any preparations. I was 8 years old!

I was a pupil when Dr Wilkie took over as Headmistress. I remember for one year we were known as Hilton PLC. The move from Hilton to the *Birida* location must have been very carefully planned and organised. I have no memories of upsets, disruptions or any worries.

Miss Ashworth then became our Headmistress and we were just PLC. We had Assembly every morning in the school hall before we went to our classes; all the school pupils attended Assembly. The Headmistress led it; a prayer, a hymn, bible reading, announcements. Miss Ashworth wore her gown. All pupils who learnt piano had to have a turn at playing the hymn to be sung by all the pupils and staff. I can remember when it was my turn I was so very nervous and frightened.

I was always a day girl and never a boarder. At morning tea I can remember the boarders queueing up to get their slice of bread, normally brown, thick and spread with melon jam. Never cut into two or four, they were just given this large thick slice of bread with the jam.

Also at morning tea two boarders could often be seen peeling potatoes from a huge container and putting them into another huge container of water.

We loved it when Sydney boys' boarding schools came to Armidale to play TAS (The Armidale School) sports. It would mean a dance at TAS one of the nights. We had to wear our school uniform of black velvet frocks with white collar and our usual brown school shoes. The TAS boys called us 'The Black Crows'. I remember having to walk past Miss Ashworth before going over to TAS while she inspected each of us to make sure we were not wearing makeup. We used to sing:

Knox, Scots, Newington, Shore.
Grammar, Barker, Kings.

On VP Day (Victory in the Pacific) on 15th August 1945, Armidale celebrated by gathering in Central Park. It must have been large because all the schools went. PLC walked down from the school to the park in crocodile, two girls abreast, keeping to the inside fences so others could pass; well-dressed of course and complete with hats and gloves. I was walking with my best friend Shirley Purkiss. As we were about to cross the road (Faulkner Street) to enter the park, our Head Prefect, Margaret McBean came and called Shirley out of line and took her away. It did puzzle me.

At the end of the service in Central Park and around the war memorial it was announced there had been a car accident and Mr Purkiss, Shirley's dad, had been killed. The passengers in the car, Sonny Macarthur, Charles Purkiss and Fred Antill, all ex-servicemen, were to have led the march. Mr Purkiss was thrown out of the car and the only one killed. My parents were at the service and when I arrived home my mother said, 'We have to go down and see Mrs Purkiss straight away.'

I remember very clearly saying, 'What will I say?'

It was very, very sad because Shirley also had a brother, Vince. There had been just the two of them in the family and Vince had joined the Air Force, but was killed in the war.

[Ed. In other reminisces of this day, Shirley is mentioned as Head Prefect. Shirley did become Head Girl the following year and this minor discrepancy is due to the vagaries of memory.]

During the war years it must have been difficult getting staff. I know a Maths teacher was shared with TAS. With clothing coupons new clothes were a luxury. Recently I saw my old school jumper. It has knitted patches in the elbows and then these were darned.

I always remember that wherever we were, if *God save the King* was played, it didn't matter what we were doing, we were taught at school to stand absolutely perfectly still at attention, arms by the sides and looking ahead. There was enormous respect for our anthem.

Another vivid memory I have is of an incident where I was in trouble. I was walking in Beardy Street, the shopping centre between Marsh and Faulkner Streets in school uniform with my hat on but no gloves. Head Prefect, Margaret McBean saw me and said she would see me next morning at school. I reported to her and she said I had to have a detention which I expected. My detention was to learn and memorise a very large number of verses from a Chapter in the Bible and then go back for her to test me. I have forgotten what it was now but I can remember for years later I would cringe when I heard that bible reading in church.

I was Captain of my House, *Gregory* in my senior year and was fortunate to have as my Vice-Captain, Trish Parr who was in my class and a boarder. Trish married Nigel Lovell and became Mistress Pat in the show *Mr Squiggle (*a TV puppet show for children*)*. She was also producer on the classic Australian movies, *Picnic at Hanging Rock* and *Gallipoli*. I was fortunate because she organised our House concerts which we had to produce for the school each term. Trish came back many years later to give the address at Speech Day for the present school but held at the university.

I loved my school years starting at Hilton then Hilton PLC and then PLC. It was the only school I attended from Kindergarten to the Leaving Certificate. They were very happy years, very smooth and uncomplicated and I made many beautiful friends and have enjoyed these friendships and companionships all my life.

My best wishes to the present and future students and I am sure you will enjoy our lovely school as much as I did.

Betty Joyce (née Harden) mid 1930s-1945

I went to school at Hilton for one year as a day pupil, unable to board until 7-years old. When PLC took over I stayed at the school until 1945.

I had two sisters Joy (two years older) and Anne (nine years younger). We were all boarders as we lived out of town. Joy and Anne left after the Intermediate Certificate.

I moved into *Birida*, Main House and stayed there until I left school. *Birida* is a lovely old house with a large outside area about it.

There were three areas of accommodation. In our dormitory we each had a bed and wardrobe. Any talking after lights out, if you were caught, you had to stand outside your dormitory until the teacher told you that you could go back to bed.

Our showers were supervised and we washed our hair on Saturdays. The laundry was all done for you, but there was a limited amount of ironing. I recall a sick bay with two beds and a 'Sister' nearby.

Later, I became a prefect and had jobs to do. Some students had to pass out the meals once a day. Students took turns to have lunch with the Principal at various times. The food was basic, for example no butter but dripping instead. I liked it! As I liked school; plenty of sport but, naturally, I also liked to get home.

There was Assembly twice a day and church on Sunday. Once a month you could go to your own church. We were Church of England so I went to St Peter's Cathedral. Saturday afternoon was spare time; sport practice, netball and the like. We had swimming and athletics carnivals. There was the occasional dance with TAS. We went to the movies at the picture theatre occasionally when a suitable film came along.

On Sunday night First Year and up went to the Headmistress's lounge where she read us a book. I can remember Miss Ashworth. Also on Sunday afternoons, if desired you could have a bag of lollies. Every term there was a long weekend when you could go home.

There were four Houses and each of us belonged to one. They were *Macquarie*, *Forrest*, *Gregory* and *Wentworth*. Sisters had to be in the same House. I was Captain of *Macquarie* in my last year.

The only times we were allowed 'down the street' was to go to the doctor or dentist, always supervised by a teacher. We wore full uniform, hat and gloves if going out.

After PLC I did nurse training at RPA Hospital, obstetrics at King George V Hospital and mental health at Gladesville Hospital.

Nancye Rew (née Pullen) 1942-1946

I came to PLC in 1942 as a Scholarship Girl from primary school in Tenterfield where there was no senior high school.

The first year I was a day girl, staying with my aunt and uncle, Dr and Mrs Hugh Harris. Their daughter, Pamela, ten or so years older than me had been to Hilton.

These of course, were the war years which coloured our lives, including trenches dug in the school grounds and air-raid drill with a rubber clenched between our teeth to take the shock of any falling bombs.

The school building was very new, with junior school classrooms, toilets, assembly hall and Headmistress's office on the ground floor and senior classes, library and staff room upstairs. I still hate walking down stairs after memories of having to walk down and upstairs with a book on my head to improve posture.

When I became a boarder in 1943, our dormitory was a long glassed-in room with hand basins, showers and toilets next door. In later years we moved to the open verandah at the front of the building. Our wet towels hanging on the ends of our beds became stiff with frost in the winter. I think I had a smaller room in my final year when I became Head Boarder. It was my job to organise a roster for peeling the potatoes.

After school we lined up each day for a slice of bread and jam served out of the kitchen window. The jam came in kerosene tins, usually apricot or melon and lemon, which I hated. I equally hated to see the butcher arrive with trays of tripe.

We also had to take it in turns to sit at the Headmistress's table for dinner. Miss Ashworth was a severe Headmistress. On Saturday afternoons we were not allowed to enter the dormitories. One day I bravely crept in and Miss Ashworth, who had rather beautiful white hair worn in a bun, was sitting there, in the sun, hair flying free to dry. I fled and the matter was never mentioned.

When the war ended we were all called into the assembly room to be given the news. Miss Ashworth told us the way to celebrate was to continue with our schoolwork. There was mutiny. We grabbed metal garbage tin lids and paraded around the school banging them like drums. Most of us had close family members involved in the war. Shirley Purkiss lost her brother during the war and my brother was in Canada learning to fly for the RAAF. The celebrations continued. We invited TAS boys to come to a dance and our Deputy Headmistress played the piano for that. Miss Ashworth made a short appearance.

During the war, when the Japanese invaded Sydney Harbour with mini submarines, Armidale was designated a 'safe city', so we had evacuees from many Sydney schools and I got to know the uniforms of most of them: SCEGGS; PLC Pymble; PLC Croydon; Ascham; MLC Burwood; Kambala; etc. As soon as the war ended they went home and our final year class was quite small.

Our uniforms consisted of summer and winter wear. As boarders, we showered each afternoon and changed into 'prep' dresses. We also had formal wear to go to church on Sundays. Funnily enough, I can't remember any of the uniform except for a white dress with a big green bow and our black velvet dresses with white lace collar. One social event I remember well was when TAS was hosting Kings for a football match and PLC and NEGS (the New England Gils' School) were invited to provide partners for a dance. The girls from NEGS wore party dresses and PLC girls lined up like crows in their black velvet dresses. You can imagine who got most of the dances.

In retrospect, in some ways, because of the war the quality of our teaching was not the best. We did not have a laboratory and physiology was the only science subject. Our French teacher was a German evacuee and our oral understanding was minimal. I did Geography Honours for the Leaving Certificate and only got a B. When my father approached Miss Ashworth about that she said it was because I was taught by an undergraduate. I did Geography because I liked drawing maps. Miss Ashworth had wanted me to do History Honours which was her subject along with English.

Maths was a problem. The only Maths teacher we had was Mr Mottershead who came over from TAS one night per week and said, 'If you want to learn Maths sit up the front, otherwise stay at the back and do crosswords.'

I still love crosswords.

It didn't help that he had a permanent sniff.

Art was my favourite subject. Our teacher was Aldyth Deer who taught me to **SEE**. For example, 'See how the shadow of the tree goes round' and again with an old master, 'Look at that red skirt'. Having won the school Art Prize in 1944, I had to drop Art completely as it was not a matriculation subject. Miss Deer was very upset.

I have since become an artist, am a Life Member of the Wagga Wagga Art Society, won many prizes and exhibited widely including Sydney, Melbourne and our home region, with four solo exhibitions in Wagga Wagga.

I did a BA and Litt B by correspondence through the University of New England (UNE) and made contact with my Armidale friends including Dorothy McRae (Curtis) and the late Joy Ramsay.

I have also had contact in Sydney with Shirley Russel (Purkiss) and Patricia Lovell (Parr) the latter of *Mr Squiggle* fame on the ABC. These two are no longer with us and I'm in my 91st year.

My religious education was coloured by the Reverend Nelson Benzely who was the minister at Armidale's Presbyterian Church where the whole school went for a Church Parade once per month.

I was an Anglican and on Fridays for Scripture we were taught by a Canon from the Armidale Cathedral who did not impress (or did) by talks of the 'sinful lusts of the flesh'. I really didn't know what he was talking about, but I didn't like it. Down the hall we could hear the laughs when Nelson Benzley read them the story of *Lassie Come Home*. When I met my future husband Ken, his father was an Elder in the Burwood Presbyterian Church where Nelson Benzley was the minister. We were married by him there in 1954.

We were taken to the Town Hall when The Sydney Symphony Orchestra came to town. The Borovansky Ballet also came and I remember their rendition of *Blue Danube* with waves of dancing in costumes of different blues. We also went to see leading male Australian tennis players who gave demonstration matches. My school report always said, 'Should play more tennis'. On Sundays after church we went on crocodile walks around the city.

On Saturday nights we danced with each other. I could play, vamping by ear, dance music. Those who learnt piano didn't learn how to play that sort of music.

One day we were taken to a local swimming hole for a picnic and got into trouble for skinny dipping.

PLC must have influenced me regarding the importance of women in society and the issue of feminism. During my tenure as Lecturer in Sociology at the Riverina College of Education (now Charles Sturt University) in the late 70s and early 80s, I contributed a chapter on Women in Local Organisations for Professor H.E. Oxley for the 2nd edition of *Mateship in Local Organisations,* 1978, University of Queensland Press. I also contributed Women In Rural Australia for a book edited by Kerry James, 1989, University of Queensland Press. The subject of my Litt B thesis was based on the Politics of Social Welfare especially during the Whitlam years.

I have had a fortunate life; a librarian in the City of Sydney Library in the beautiful Queen Victoria Building; trained as a nurse and graduated from Royal Prince Alfred Hospital; married Ken, a doctor, went to New Zealand before travel to the UK for my husband's specialist studies in Obstetrics and Gynaecology; had three children; set up a successful medical practice in Wagga Wagga and Ken became a foundation member of the Royal Australian College of Obstetrics and Gynaecology.

Barbara Brett 1944-1948

My boarding years at *Birida* got off to a rocky start which was disastrous for me, a shy country girl, as two of us were separated from everyone coming into South Dorm. There wasn't enough room for us all, someone got the numbers wrong, so two of us were sent down to Junior House with the little kids, under the watchful eye of 'Willie Wire Whiskers' (Miss Williams). It was hard to form friendships and develop a routine, but things got better. We progressed to *Birida* and into, not South Dorm, but 'The Back Hole', a small room with a window overlooking North Dorm. Still isolated but at least we were in Main House.

I eventually made South Dorm at the beginning of Term 2 and life began. Although I had to behave as my bed was right under Hammy's window which opened onto our verandah sleep out.
[Ed. Hammy was companion to the Headmistress].

There were plenty of rules; showers at night before tea and in trouble if you were late to the Dining Room. We could wash our hair on Saturday mornings, plus our socks.

Every morning we had to be up, out and into the gym for early morning drill (exercises) which finished with all of us running around the block quite a distance.

I was a member of the A Basketball Team (now called netball), was goalie so instead of having to do drill I was sent up to the basketball courts to practice my goaling.

During the week after tea was 'Prep' until 8.00 pm and later as a Senior until 9.00 pm. Also we had a roster as to who was going to supervise the First, Second and Third Years (for their own Prep). We were allowed a cup of cocoa in the kitchen on our way from Prep to our Dorm. The cocoa was absolutely terrible. Mrs. Price, our cook, was not good; burnt porridge and pea soup. I have never eaten melon and lemon jam since my school days. Brown ants used to invade the kitchen and the jam. To try and make us eat it, Mrs. P. mixed the melon and lemon jam with the marmalade which we did all eat, but the mixture didn't work for me.

We lined up at the kitchen window for morning tea of slices of bread and jam and afternoon tea was a biscuit and a piece of fruit supplied by our parents. On Sundays we got a piece of cake for afternoon tea after a lunch of roast meat and vegetables. I must admit it was wartime and food rationing, so we were lucky with what we did get.

We were very rarely allowed down the street during term time. If we did go it was wearing full uniform, including our hats and gloves and we were escorted by a prefect.

Every Sunday we went to church, me to St Peter's Cathedral for the 9.30 am service. We Anglicans would be coming home as the Presbyterians were walking down to St Paul's 11.00 am service. Sunday night we gathered in Miss Ashworth's drawing room to be read a story, usually a book read over a number of Sundays. Once a week, on Friday mornings, we walked down to the town baths which were shut to the public while we had a couple of hours in the pool. It was the same place where our Swimming Carnival was held each year. Our Athletics Carnival was usually held on the Rugby League Football ground near the swimming pool. I enjoyed my tennis, basketball and ball games but not swimming, which I always regretted not learning.

The dances we had with TAS boys were quite forgettable to me. We had to share with NEGS, our rivals and they always arrived in 'coloured' clothes, make-up, etc. and we would arrive in our black velvet dresses, no make-up. I think Miss Ashworth thought we would all end up pregnant if we dared to dress up or look sideways at a boy.

We always had a Boarders' Picnic which I quite enjoyed although here again we were strictly supervised and laden with rules - no swimming, no paddling, no wandering off, etc.

Mid Terms were always very welcome as I could go home for the weekend. Home was local and not far from town.

As it was wartime staff shortages came into play so the boarders were rostered to do the washing up, two to a shift. Another job was peeling the potatoes - a good detention exercise on occasion. I think sometimes the peel was thicker than the potato and often I wonder whether it was a practical exercise. In the winter time it was a very popular chore as we peeled them sitting in the boiler room, a lovely warm spot.

We were also rostered to wait on tables in the Dining Room; it had to be done properly. Also, we were rostered to sit at the Headmistress's table at lunch time for a week. I dreaded this as we had to eat everything on our plate, ugh!

I liked East Dorm but North Dorm was a shock—so cold with only canvas blinds for shelter from the weather. The route from our dormitory to our showers and toilets was a bit hazardous as we had to go through part of Main Hall past 'Ash's' quarters. She and Hammy always knew who was running late for tea.

The 'hospital' was an old cottage converted to a ward, dispensary and flat for Sister. At the end of the verandah was our laundry collection room. We seemed to be fairly healthy except once there was an epidemic of conjunctivitis. I became a victim and ended up in South Dorm which became an isolation ward.

Peggy Craddock (née Wilkinson) 1945-1949

When we arrived at what was then called First Year, and looking forward to finishing with the Leaving Certificate, we were told we'd be ending our time at PLC on the 'Promised Land'. This seemed to disappear further into the future as each year finished. After the Leaving Certificate we Fifth Formers were allowed to take a picnic lunch and walk in mufti in that magical? place, unsupervised!

I arrived at the Brown Street residence on the Armidale to Grafton bus from the Orphanage at Grafton having won a State Bursary and the scholarship to PLC. My teacher at South Grafton Public was brilliant;

six of my class were awarded State Bursaries one coming second in the exam.

I was absolutely terrified. Before I left the orphanage I was warned, as usual, that everything would go wrong, I was useless and everyone would hate me because I would cause disasters to happen. Having that drummed into you several times a day accompanied by beltings with the broomstick takes its toll.

So it was that I arrived very malnourished and was made to stand in the dining room and swallow ghastly medication to improve my health. When the end of the Pacific War was in sight my malnourishment caught up with me and I was covered in boils. I was made to lie on my stomach in the Assembly Hall, listening to the radio and to give the news to Miss Ashworth. The news came when we were in Prep to general rejoicing. We joined the Victory Parade, but the Head Prefect's father was killed in a car accident on the way to joining it. The whole school went into mourning.

A very special memory is when each school had to provide special entertainment for a city-wide celebration. In the Town Hall, Nina Sourry and Pam Saunders, both day girls, performed a brilliant pas de deux choreographed by the sports mistress. The crowd went wild and thereafter they were asked to repeat it for special occasions. We were all so proud of them, marvelling at the skill and beauty; it was truly glorious. Every time I hear that music I am taken back to that evening and see in my mind's eye that stunning performance.

Each class in turn would provide an entertainment in the gym on Saturday evenings.

We lined up at the kitchen window at recess for brown bread and plum jam. The running around the block before breakfast each morning was not enjoyed much in the Armidale winter. One feature everyone would remember was the short sheeting of beds accompanied by holly leaves from the little park behind the tennis courts.

Mary Ranger and I were punished for reading after lights out, using a torch. Another time, having provided one of the ribbons which I used on my former plaits to tie Miss Ashworth's birthday package, I was caught reading again and forbidden to go to her birthday party.

The 1945 First Year class surely remember the 'diffusion and osmosis' experiment sitting forlornly on a table in the classroom. After many days of failure, the whole class decided to covertly give it a helping hand. Result? The teacher was surprised at how well it worked! Girls will be girls.

Another memory is the many performances of classical music we attended in the Town Hall. There were many such visits and we were privileged to go.

I guess everyone remembers the timed 'three minute' showers and the chicken pox and conjunctivitis outbreaks where those affected went to sick bay under the care of Matron.

I recall listening on the radio to the description of the wedding of then Princess Elizabeth to Prince Phillip.

We sometimes watched football matches at TAS between them and city boarding schools and went to dances at TAS that evening. On one occasion we hosted the players to a dance in the Assembly Hall.

Miss Ashworth's sitting room became an emergency bedroom for some of the South Dorm residents when the whole of the dorm had to be evacuated. Heavy snow had blocked the gutters and the dorm was flooded. The girls rolled up bedding and went to find a dry place. The power failed and, as one evacuee described it, a Florence Nightingale was appointed and she held a lit hurricane lantern to guide her cohorts to 'dry land'. (August 26, 1949.)

One evening, sitting in Prep in the 6A classroom, we heard a very loud crack. A huge branch of the beautiful wattle tree snapped off due to the weight of snow.

On one journey back to school on the Woodward and Purkiss bus, those of us who travelled that day were alarmed about the smokey air. Then on the winding road we came upon the bushfire. The driver was absolutely amazing. He got us through and delivered the students to their various schools in town.

Our Leaving Certificate oral French exam was conducted by the UNE French lecturer. I think we all passed even though we were so nervous.

Mary Ranger and I had to go up to Armidale Teachers' College to be interviewed as we were both applying to do teacher training. I became a Teacher Librarian.

Some pupils I remember and some I've come across since leaving. I frequently came into contact with Peggy Shannon during my time as Teacher Librarian at Matthew Pearce school at Baulkam Hills where she was a much admired mayor. We shared lots of memories, I sadly recently sent news of her passing to *Green Tartan*. (The PLC Armidale bi-annual magazine).

I caught up with Barbara Strachan (Brown) in Moree when she enrolled her grandson into the library at Moree Primary School and was reminded that I used to correct her spelling. When she was doing correspondence school, she and her brother would write the spelling test words on the ceiling and copy them when her mother tested them.

My very best wishes for the continued success of the school.

Rosemary Perrott-Russell (née Perrott) 1949-1954

These are my memories of PLC in Brown Street, which I attended for six years, from 1949 to 1954.

Miss Buchan would read a story to those boarders who wanted to attend, I don't think it was compulsory, but I remember she read the book, *The Thirty Nine Steps* by John Buchan. I was enthralled and have bought most of John Buchan's books.

Miss Williams would take us down to St. Peter's Cathedral on some Sundays as there were a few of us who were members of the Church of England. There were some Sundays we went to the Presbyterian Church and I was so bored I would count certain words the minister used frequently.

I remember doing the washing of a Saturday in the copper. On one occasion, along with the socks and hankies we boiled a tin of condensed milk so we had caramel to eat.

In the afternoons when school had finished we would be given bread and jam to eat and I remember we would try to toast this on the radiator.

During the winter we would have to run in the mornings, before lessons commenced, around the block. This was miserable and rather trying for me as I came up from the warm and hot coastal area to a cold tablelands winter.

We had, on odd occasions, dances with the TAS boys. I was so shy that I put the boys off dancing with me. It was not to my liking being a wall flower.

I remember when sleeping on the open veranda with a number of others in the main building, a man got into the dormitory and tried to get into bed with one of the girls; it wasn't me.

We would sit on our rugs outside on the weekends or play tennis or some other game.

We did have midnight feasts. I was not the instigator. I was more of a follower.

I remember being sent out of assembly because I was talking. I was punished by being made to learn, off by heart, the hymn that was sung 'Dear Lord and Father of mankind, forgive our foolish ways'.

I recall during my last exams being encouraged to take illegal drugs by one or more of my fellow students; they were to keep us awake to study, but I never did. I was told by my mother I would be sorry in later life for not studying hard, she was right.

I was teased by some of the students but I coped.

I recall being given the polio vaccine when one of the PLC students contracted it.

Pam Harvey (née Davidson) 1947-1951

Pam died in 2019 and these reminisces are contributed by John, her husband[Ed.].

I am in receipt of your letter requesting memories of *Birida* days of PLC. Unfortunately when Pam passed away last year, those memories went with her. She often spoke of living in the cottages which were very cold with little or no heating. The girls brought brown paper to put between the blankets and wore clothes on top of their pyjamas to go to bed. Pam attended PLC from 1947 to 1951. To put that in perspective, conditions were much the same at Farrer, which I attended from 1944 to 1948.

Pam told of the long trips home at holiday time on Mrs. Hong's Bundarra mail truck which also delivered bread. There were 94 mail boxes between Armidale and the Davidson property and the young passenger was expected to jump out to place the parcel in the box.

Janice Holcombe (née Todd) 1947-55

I attended PLC Armidale from 3rd Class to 5th Year or Leaving year. I fully remember when my sister Helen and I first went to PLC not knowing anyone and feeling completely lost.

A girl who was in a class below Helen came and talked to us which was marvellous and we gradually got to know more girls. We were day girls. Assembly was at 9.00 am each morning. We caught a bus which came from Uralla to Armidale and by the time we arrived at school Assembly was in, so we had to stand outside Miss Ashworth's office and say we were late due to the bus being late. Later we bought bikes and rode them to school and made it to Assembly, which was much better.

We always had to wear our hats and gloves when in uniform; trouble awaited us if we didn't have them on. The boarders ran around the block first thing in the morning. At morning tea the boarders lined up for bread and jam; day girls took their own.

There were three boarding houses, Main House, Junior House and Prep House. The rules were strict. At Brown Street there were basketball (netball) courts and four tennis courts. The school had land up North Hill (the 'Promised Land') and later the school moved up to the Promised Land and the Brown Street buildings were all sold.

On Sunday mornings the boarders went to St. Paul's Presbyterian church and the rest of the day was spent reading in the grounds or playing tennis.

Mid-terms were popular and boarders spent these weekend breaks with families of day girls or of girls who lived close to Armidale. We enjoyed sport and ball games. On Friday mornings in the warmer days, the school went to the baths and learnt to swim; we would walk to the baths, do the swimming and walk back to the school.

Miss Drummond was my teacher in 3rd and 4th Classes. She taught us to sew by hand and we all loved her.

Our four Houses, *Wentworth, Macquarie, Gregory* and. *Forrest* were called after explorers who opened up the land; we barracked hard and loud for our House to win at the Sports and Swimming Carnivals.

In some winter holidays I went with my school friend Nancye McDonald on the train to Moree to be met by her parents and taken to their property, 'Gilroy' where we spent many happy days riding horses and visiting their neighbours.

I have many happy memories of my days at PLC Armidale.

Laurel McCosker (née Cole) 1945-1947

I was at PLC, 110 Brown Street from 1945-1947. I lived at Delungra, NSW and I'd never heard of Armidale!

My most vivid memory was the day war ended. The boys from TAS came over on bikes with rolls of toilet paper; there was paper everywhere.

A sad thing happened that day. Our lovely Head Girl's father was killed. He was called Chook Purkiss. We were so sorry for all the family. Her name was Shirley.

Everything changed after that. The juniors had to peel the potatoes- four gallon bucket fulls. We sat in the boiler room. I loved the company of the girls as I only had a brother.

We did P.E., played tennis and basketball (they call it netball now). We washed our heads and socks on Saturday morning. We could wear normal clothes on Saturday and we'd sit on our big rugs on the lawn.

I learnt music from Miss Wharton. I loved her. I'd learnt music before and could play by ear. Also we played the hymn for evening and morning prayers

We had some girls from Newcastle and Sydney, Armidale being called safer than the coast. My first year was spent in Junior House. Miss Williams and Miss Hamilton were in charge.

We wore black velvet frocks with lace collars and cuffs to dinner at night. In summer time there was a green prep. frock and Sunday church wear was a white frock with a green pussy bow. I still have my bow. For winter there was a green overcoat.

There were about 20 girls in my class and I can remember most of their names.

Maureen Smith 1948-50s

The kitchen lady couldn't find the plug to the wash-up sink and appealed to us to look for it. Days passed without its appearance. Then, one day she told us in triumph that she had found it. Oh, good, we said, where?

At the bottom of the rhubarb saucepan, was the reply.

Jean Ferguson (née Muir) 1946-1954

I started in Fourth Class, was 9-years old and the teacher had four classes of small girls to educate. There were three others in my class, and I was boarding at Prep House with the other boarders who were in the primary school. A house mistress and another teacher lived at Prep House with us.

We wore bottle green tunics with three box pleats front and back and a white blouse and green tie to school (I had to learn to tie a tie). In winter the tunics were made of serge and in summer tobralco, a much lighter fabric. At night in winter for the evening meal we wore a black velvet dress. Velvet was not available when I started at PLC as we still had rationing, but my dress was of a woollen material and the dress had a white collar. We did have a green cotton dress for dinner at night in the summer.

For church on Sunday during summer we wore a white dress with a floppy bottle green bow at the neck. The Presbyterians walked to church a few blocks from the school, two abreast to the service at 11am on Sundays. We had a panama hat to wear on formal occasions in summer, and in winter it was a velour hat (I think). We also had a bottle green blazer and a jumper as part of our uniform. I do remember it was difficult to get all the uniform together just after the war. Over the years there have been a number of changes to the uniform. The garment I remember most is the suit which was of course bottle green.

During the week we had prayers in the Assembly Hall in the morning before school started and at night before we did our prep. The Headmistress always took Assembly and music students played the piano for hymns. In the winter getting up to practice the piano at 6am it could be very cold. We had five special music rooms with a piano in each and there were various pianos in other areas of the school which were also used. We had a sports teacher who came from the Swords Club in Sydney (I doubt if it exists now) and each class had two periods each week of exercises and learning games etc. We loved it.

As we progressed through the school, my class became quite large and in 1953 there were 17 who sat for the Leaving Certificate. I stayed until 1954.

Most of us have kept in touch with school friends throughout our lives but the numbers are thinning now. The library books we had at PLC in those days were quite different to the ones that would be there now. I can remember someone telling me that the best way to choose a 'good book' was to get one that was very tatty.

Preparing to join the town march celebrating the Victory in the Pacific (VP Day). *Photo: Nancye Rew (née Pullen).*

Prefects 1944 with Miss Ashworth, Headmistress
L-R: Margaret Weiss, Peggy Shannon, Barbara Brett, Betty Henderson, Patti Mott, Jean Trimble. Front- Miss Clarice Ashworth. *Photo: Barbara Brett.*

Main House with the latticed North Dorm, 1953.
Photo: Christine Perrott (née Ewing).

Main House and classroom block, 1940, gardens being prepared.
Photo: PLC Archives.

Junior House. *Photo: Barbara McHattan (née Reid).*

School classroom block. *Photo: Barbara McHattan (née Reid).*

Miss Ashworth, Headmistress.
Photo: PLC Archives.

Winter tunic. *Photo: PLC Archives.*

Summer tunic.
Photo: Christine Perrott (née Ewing).

Frock for Prep and weekends.
Photo: Christine Perrott (née Ewing).

School Suit. *Photo: PLC Archives.*

Winter velour hat worn by Mrs Jean Thorpe, watching tennis.
Photo: Christine Perrott (née Ewing).

White formal summer and church dress, blazer, hat and gloves. L-R Heather Rodgers, Robyn McGuffike, Jan Weatherburn, Liz Manuel. *Photo: PLC Archives.*

Tunic with Blazer and tie. *Photo: PLC Archives.*

PART TWO

The Early 1950s

Introduction

In the early 1950s Australia continued to welcome post-war immigrants. At least one PLC girl whose memories appear in this section came to Australia in this program.

1950 was a year of climate disasters which included a cyclone in northern NSW resulting in 7 deaths plus 26 deaths from severe gales, floods and high seas. Australia started sending ground troops to Korea.

The Aboriginal tenor Harold Blair performed in Armidale Town Hall in 1951 as part of his concert tour program. Polio was still raging and caused 121 deaths Australia-wide. The bikini appeared, shocking beach goers, and Armidale's Powerhouse closed so that its electricity had to come from Tamworth's Powerhouse.

Britain began its years of atomic bomb testing in Australia, but most Australians knew nothing about it as it was so hush-hush. King George VI died in February 1952 and some of the families of PLC girls were affected by the serious flooding of all major NSW rivers that summer.

The coronation of Queen Elizabeth II in June 1953 caused great excitement and the collection of publications full of coloured photos of the event and the Royal Family was popular. Some of the shine of the year was taken away when two trains collided in Sydney injuring 748 people.

In 1954 the population of Armidale was 7,845. The University of New England (UNE) became autonomous from the University of Sydney. Gara Dam was built to add to Armidale's water security.

Again there was a climate catastrophe in NSW; this time a cyclone hit the Northern Rivers area killing 26. The visit to Australia of the new Queen and her husband, Prince Phillip took precedence in engaging the populace over the strange Petrov spy affair.

Dinah Roepers (née Burnett) 1952-1953

I was a boarder at PLC Armidale for two years, 1952-1953. At the time, my family lived in Lismore. I had always wanted to go to boarding school so now was my chance and I didn't regret a minute of that time. I would have to say that my education during that period may have been more productive at Lismore High, but nothing could replace the experience of being a boarder for those two years.

At that time, there were three boarding houses: Prep, Junior and Main (*Birida*). There were just over 100 boarders and about 30 day girls from memory. There was an old house (*Birida*) joined together with land behind where there were tennis and basketball (netball) courts. The school block (now an aged care facility) was built on some of that land. There was a gym. During my tenure, a new dining room and kitchen were built behind Main House. The original dining room was in Main House and later turned into another dorm. There was also another cottage behind the new dining room which was the sick bay. The 'live in' mistresses lived in a cottage not far from the main school. We used to look from the school block across the city to the 'Promised Land' where the current school now sits. Prep was in the school rooms.

Miss Kathryn Buchan joined the school as Headmistress at the beginning of my first year; sadly her tenure only lasted the two years I was at PLC. She was lured back to New Zealand as Principal of Columba Girls College in Dunedin.

I always felt I was fortunate to have her for those two years. She did her best to modernise the school but I think the then School Council was difficult to move. She was able to purchase a movie projector which gave us a movie once a week. On the odd occasion when there was a significant event on in town, she arranged for us to attend. I remember going to the screening of *The Great Caruso* and a ballet. Miss Buchan also read to the 4th and 5th form girls in her sitting room on a Sunday night. It all seems a bit laughable today!

Miss Buchan brought a friend of hers to be Mistress of Main House. She was a Scottish doctor with a very broad accent. I spent one year in East Dorm and one in North Dorm. East Dorm was closed in but North Dorm wasn't; we had roll-up blinds for privacy. They did little to keep the cold out! In both cases, beds were arranged head to toe around the perimeter of the verandah with an attached dressing room, with a drawer and hanging space each. I don't think that was heated but we all survived. Doonas didn't exist then.

I seem to remember having seven blankets on my bed. During this time, we had a bit of 'dorm drama'; we had an intruder get into South Dorm. Fortunately he did no harm and was eventually caught sitting in the tree outside North Dorm some weeks down the track. We often wondered what he might have made of the conversations emanating from the dorm!

Uniforms for particular times were strictly adhered to; gloves, hats, stockings. Breaking bounds was strictly prohibited. Going to church or anywhere else was in crocodile fashion, two abreast. You moved off the footpath and opened doors for others. You didn't ask for something at the dining table; you enquired whether another person wanted the butter and hoped they got the message that you did!

Morning and afternoon tea comprised bread and jam, with the bread, more often than not, being quite stale. I don't remember what we had to drink, if anything. Food in the new dining room with a new chef was an improvement, but it has taken me fifty years to rediscover and enjoy bread and butter pudding.

Sunday church was of course a must. The seniors sat in the choir seats which gave us an overview of the rest of the girls. I think on occasions we sang during the service. I went to PLC with a church background so didn't find that difficult, but I would have to say the minister at that time didn't exactly inspire. However, my faith remains strong and I have always had, as I have now, an active role in the church.

Recreation and spare time was largely of one's own making. There was tennis, soft ball and basketball, but sitting on a rug in the sunshine was the go in the weekend. Although we did have organised sports and swimming carnivals.

We also had the occasional dance with boys from TAS. There was one mid-term break each term. Where families lived nearby, girls went home, taking friends who had no other option with them. I was fortunate to have family friends on a farm near Woolbrook and always went there for my mid-term breaks.

I think the greatest lesson I took from my time at PLC was to learn to live with, and be considerate of, others who came from so many different backgrounds. Most of all, I retain friendships from that time which are very important to me. I can't say my time at PLC helped me determine what I wanted to do with my life; I did learn typing from the school secretary and eventually that is the path I followed; one of secretarial and administration.

The years following PLC have been productive and interesting. My time at the school gave me the confidence to give things a go, even though I felt ill equipped to do a particular job. With the doing, my confidence grew, enabling me to do things and go places I never dreamt I could or would. That learning to live with others also helped me when I married (at 43), a widower with three daughters.

My two years at PLC were the happiest of my school life and I don't regret a minute of that time. I am very grateful to my parents who made great sacrifices to allow me to follow my dream of going to boarding school.

Gweneth Berman (née McKenzie)
1949-1951

I was a day girl at PLC when it was at Brown Street, thus I didn't live in *Birida*, but I did spend one night there in 1949 when Dumaresq Creek flooded and we couldn't get home to North Hill.

Miss Ashworth was the Headmistress. She was an imposing figure, a most impressive lady.

I really loved my time at PLC. I made long lasting friendships and am still in touch with some of my classmates. Sadly, several have passed away. I feel that values that were instilled in me at home were reinforced at school and have stayed with me to this day.

Many girls had music lessons during school hours. We went out of the school grounds, across the street to the homes of Miss Wharton and her sister Mrs Hutton, or to Mrs Craigie, a whole block away, quite unaccompanied! I can't imagine that being allowed today.

I am still teaching music after a long career as a secondary school teacher and am well acquainted with all the Working with Children rules we have to follow now. Miss Wharton was my piano teacher. She played the organ at the Presbyterian church and she introduced me to pipe organ playing; a wonderful experience. I played for services there for about 18 years before we left Armidale and am still playing on a regular basis, about 70 years later, unfortunately not a pipe organ.

We had a roster at PLC for hymn playing for Morning Assembly.

I did some teaching at PLC, part time during my studies at UNE and full time in 1957. I then had a break while having my children and returned to teaching in the new school (on the Promised Land) in 1964. This continued until 1967 when we left Armidale for Wellington.

We often had 'home grown' performances on Saturday nights. I particularly remember my class performing a little operetta called *Antonio*. The music actually featured well known tunes from opera so we were quite ambitious. We also performed an operetta based on Shakespeare's *Macbeth* written by my father Dr K McKenzie (later chairman of PLC Board.) It featured music from Gilbert and Sullivan, for example, *'Three little Scottish witches we'* instead of *'Three little Maids from school'*. We had such fun preparing and performing these items. I have gone on to play for many town and school musicals especially in Wellington and Maclean.

So you can see my time at PLC has had a great effect on my life since then.

I did put together a booklet on what my classmates did after leaving school. The school should have a copy of it.

Gerlinde Spencer (née Braunschweig) 1951-52

What a wonderful two years of shelter and comfort, and to my surprise academic achievement, this financial sacrifice by my parents gave me. To be immersed in English (no German teacher available) day and night for the whole of each twelve week term helped me to get better marks in my English than in my 1st Class Honours in German in the Leaving Certificate. I found this out much later when I had my interview with an officer of the Education Department whose job it was to follow up on students who had been granted a Commonwealth Scholarship for their tertiary education. Mind you, the snooty little man who examined my spoken German for the Leaving Certificate had threatened not to pass me because my *Hochdeutch* sounded too Austrian. I would not be surprised if he gave me a low mark.

To get back to PLC and its opportunities. First of all were the lovely girls, mostly from outlying farms within reach of Armidale on the Northern Tablelands of NSW. A few came from Sydney and the majority were boarders who did not go home except for a mid-term weekend in the winter term and the school holidays. They were kind and unsophisticated, curious about this new girl who had been on 'the other side' during the recent World War.

The teachers were great too, if not necessarily of a high academic standard. Miss Ashworth, the Head, might be old school and imposing but she was wise enough to assign me to my dear 'Fatty' with whom I roomed on my own for the whole of first term. Fatty (Mary White) had been a boarder at PLC since she was six, as her parent's farm at Boggabri was a long way from civilisation, so she knew the ropes well and truly. She was big and strong and used to give me spontaneous piggy back rides which I loved despite my 15 years. These were the days before hugging became a socially acceptable way of showing affection, so they were great.

Early on I overheard the teachers worrying about me because some of the girls tried to taunt me by singing *Rule Britannia* and other patriotic songs in my presence. I did not tell them that because my mother was British this did not faze me one bit, but rather gave me some wry amusement. Much later I used to entertain my class during the periodic blackouts we had when back in our classroom at night doing prep (homework), by playing the German and Italian songs I had learnt on my recorder. They particularly liked *Lilli Marlene* which I sang in German.

Soon however, all this was left behind as I got more skilful at hitting a ball with an object, be it rounders or tennis; learned to dance the Scottish Highland Reel (three of us in tartan kilts and a soprano on the stage of the Armidale Town Hall, where we even did the famous Sword Dance); joined in eurhythmics (on the front lawn of the school); played the Highland Hero in a one-act play competition which we won; learned ballroom dancing with a group of boys from TAS for a winter term on Friday evenings; continued my violin lessons with a teacher in town whose cat used to leave the room when I arrived; played goal defence in inter-school netball competitions in the B team and trained for the Bronze Medal in swimming. Sadly we never got to the medal stage as there was an outbreak of polio in Armidale and the public pool was closed for the rest of the time I was there.

This was before the Sabine Polio Vaccine had been developed and there was no defence against the disease which could kill you or leave you paralysed in various limbs and/or your lungs, resulting in life in an iron lung which helped you to survive but not much else. It was and is a horrifying disease which these days can be avoided by a few drops of vaccine on the tongue. Janet Wade, a year behind me in 4th Year and destined to be Head Prefect when she got to 5th Year was diagnosed with polio while I was also in sick bay, a small cottage in the school grounds. We visited her in Armidale Hospital when she could barely move at all. It was devastating and I was grateful I had not caught the bug. Years later we met again and Ian and I were amazed at how she had triumphed over a severe disability. By that time she was married, was an ordained minister in the Uniting Church, serving a parish and as full of life as I remember her before she got ill. One of her legs and one arm dragged badly but you hardly noticed because of her ability to engage with people and what was going on. A tough life nevertheless.

Day to day life at PLC had its moments. There was the three day old, thickly sliced, horrible white bread, not to be confused with the light and fluffy milk bread of today. We, in the Senior's dining room, were sure the teachers who sat on a raised dais in the room, were served with fresh bread. So occasionally we tried to draw attention to our tough slices by bouncing them on edge on the floor beside us. As this did not get any results, not even a reprimand, we eventually resorted to collecting the bread, stuffing it down the front of our school tunics and up the sides of our elasticised green bloomers and setting off to feed the chooks in the four fowl yards at the school perimeter. To our joy we actually ran the kitchen out of stale bread and had fresh for one whole day, but for only a day as the cook must have ordered at least double. I revelled in such fun and I have no memory of anyone getting into trouble.

We had that bread for morning and afternoon tea, lavishly covered in melon and lemon jam, which most of us disliked, and no butter. Apparently there had been a mistake in the ordering of the jam which came in large kerosene tins, so we had to wait for more than one term to get a change. In the end teenage hunger prevailed and we took to scraping the jam off with our fingers into any handy garden bed before eating the bread. What bliss to be allowed to have a tucker tin once you were a prefect in 5th Year. We could feast on Vita Wheat biscuits with vegemite or peanut butter and other things that would keep without a fridge. We also had our own space in a temporary building where we'd withdraw to. Some of our free time we did use to go over and over *Richard II,* the Shakespeare play set for the Leaving, which no doubt helped my English mark in the final exams.

Our menu each week in my first year was fixed. The old cook had been there for many years and retired when Miss Ashworth did. Monday breakfast was toast, Tuesday tinned spaghetti, Wednesday toast, Thursday baked beans, Friday toast, Saturday curried sausages. Each round table of seven or eight was headed by a prefect and in my final year I discovered that we prefects worked out the seating between ourselves at the beginning of the year. This meant that if you really liked baked beans you tried to have at least one person at your table who did not, so you could have the second portion, ditto the other choices. It sounds hilarious, but food becomes quite a focus for people in institutions.

Another thing I learnt was that to be fair we sent the butter plate, containing one small piece per person, alternately to the left or to the right, seating order being fixed for the year. You were free to take the largest piece when it was your turn so that worked out about right. Fair prefects took part in this, greedy ones always took the largest piece as their right. Dinner was midday and not remarkable except for horrible milk puddings, the worst being lemon sago and custard, both firm set. Friday after Friday, every lunch time, these plates came out on tea trolleys, only to be sent back to the kitchen uneaten. The system was firmly set and not responsive to feedback. Tea was at 5.30 pm and consisted of bread, jam and cheddar cheese; an extraordinary combination to my still European palate. Not much fruit or salads and, like the diet, we grew pretty solid ourselves.

The worst meal, which could have been the best, was Sunday lunch after church. We walked to the rather lovely little Presbyterian Church in town and back again (in our best Sunday outfits) only to be greeted by the smell of boiled cabbage, whole potatoes, not browned but covered in grease, with thick brown gravy over slabs of sliced hogget roast. Some of my peers had eaten this menu for anything up to eight years of their lives. But it all ended with the appointment of Miss Buchan as our new Headmistress.

During my first year a group of us decided to do the traditional raid on the kitchen, availing ourselves of the cooked sausages before they were turned into awful curry, plus whatever else presented itself. We managed to get into the locked premises around midnight, greatly excited at our daring. Some of the cupboard doors had locks but not the huge industrial fridge; so there were the cold sausages! I think there was some fuss about the theft but no one was made to own up as far as I recall. To my mind it was wonderful 'British boarding school' stuff, like living in a book.

Our sleeping arrangements were primitive; iron bedsteads with wire base and Kapok mattresses, lumpy pillows, smooth white sheets and grey army blankets, not much defence during an Armidale winter which could go to -2°C and even produce a sprinkling of snow. All there was between us and the elements was a wooden lattice covered with climbing roses in summer. We used to go to bed wearing track suits on top of our pyjamas in winter and sit on the bed popping rose petals in summer, or in my case tapping a pet Greengrocer cicada named Rex to produce a noise at each tap. I also smuggled in a hot water bottle. That is until it leaked one night, leaving me with wet sheets and mattress. Matron was not impressed when she followed the commotion after lights out to find us draping the sheets over the wardrobe door in a vain attempt at drying them out. There went the water bottle!

Another thing we used our beds for was to dry illegal washing such as underpants under the mattress. Laundry was outsourced and strictly counted, so at period time (the era of clumsy sanitary pads and belts) three pairs of bottle green bloomers was not enough. We had to sew our hankies together at the corner (no tissues then) so they would not get lost in the wash, with the result that all of them had holes at the corners. And of course, every garment had to have a sown on tape embroidered with our name.

My first mid-term break was very special as I was invited to spend the weekend with Catherine Campbell on her parent's farm. This was bliss. The day started with a huge breakfast. Both of us sat up side by side in a big double bed and enjoyed lamb cutlets (from their own sheep), bacon and eggs, homemade marmalade and toast and tea, all lovingly served by Catherine's Mum. This was followed by a look around the immediate timber family house and yard with her Dad and a ride around the property on a pair of very easy horses - again, story book stuff which I revelled in. Catherine's Mum made an impressive lot of plain sweet biscuits, with here and there a black currant, which she rolled very thin, then cut out on the kitchen table. After baking they were stored in a huge glass jar. All new, all learning, all special.

At school I used to listen to Catherine practice the piano which she was very good at. I had learned to love classical music in Austria, so listening to her thundering out Beethoven or Rachmaninoff while I sat on the hard wooden floor of the 'music room', helped with the loss of my home country and the transition to feeling more at home in Australia. Catherine went a long way with her music professionally as an adult, but sadly had tinnitus in later years. Undaunted, she turned to writing and I am presently really enjoying her first published book.

The following year I spent the mid-term weekend with Judith McLean's family on her parent's farm in Guyra. Mid-term weekend was in winter and Guyra was a cold windy place, as was their house where the wind found its way between some of the weatherboards. The new farmhouse was almost completed and the family was really glad that this was their last winter in the old one. We still managed to have a great time however, rugged up against the cold. I was so grateful for the kindness of the Campbells and the McLeans in taking me in, as I would have had to stay at school for those weekends otherwise. Laurieton was too far away to make the trip home worthwhile and it was also a unique introduction to country Australia.

This brings me to the business of travelling to school and back each term, which was quite something. First we had to pack my 'port', as suitcases were then called, with all the paraphernalia of the school uniform. Just as well we wore ordinary clothes only to Friday night dance classes with the TAS boys during winter term each year as there was a uniform for every other occasion. Summer uniform included two green lightweight box pleated tunics and several white short sleeved shirts, green sleeveless sports shift and white polo shirt, white dress with a big green bow at the neck for church and other special occasions, a similar green frock with a white collar for after school hours, a straw hat with green band and school crest and a bottle green school blazer with pale blue trim and crest on the pocket. The inscription on the crest was *Ad Astra* roughly translated as, 'To the stars'; very noble and inspiring. Added to all these were the uncomfortable bras, some cotton singlets, bottle green bloomers (baggy underpants), white socks and hankies.

Winter uniform was suited to the cold climate of the New England plateau…and unheated rooms. Blazer, woollen jumper, wool overcoat (an expensive item), winter suit (ditto), wool serge box pleated tunic, velour hat with band (all bottle green), long sleeved white shirts and tie, brown lyle stockings with suspender belt, black velvet dress with lace collar for going to concerts in town. All this filled my big port to overflowing, except that we travelled to and from school in uniform which helped.

Irmgard joined me in my last year so we travelled together. The journey took nearly a whole day by the time Vati (Dad) drove us to Wauchope where we picked up the bus for Armidale. It was driven by a long and lanky Aussie who gave us a jovial welcome and got to know us as we went back and forth at the beginning and end of each term. Our heavy suitcases were no problem to him! We enjoyed the trip through flat farm country followed by the impressive forests as we wound our way up the steep incline to the plateau. We always stopped halfway up the climb at a lookout, where there was a small café, for tea and scones with strawberry jam and whipped cream. This was a real treat as the bus trip (no 'coaches' then) took hours.

Back at school we enjoyed our Sunday afternoon excursions to 'The Promised Land' where the new school is now long established and very lovely. It was good to have a less regimented time to walk and talk and to amuse ourselves. We would put a dent in the rounded top of our green velour winter hats so they looked more like the ones the TAS boys wore—a disreputable group! The summer straw hats were not as amenable to alterations.

When it came to boys, there was TAS, an Anglican boarding school for boys, much larger than PLC. Their sister school was NEGS and there was quite some rivalry between the two Protestant schools for the only eligible boys in town. De La Salle, the Catholic boys school, had St Ursula's girls to connect with and in those days the separation between Catholic and Protestant was an unpleasant constant. Our main advantage over NEGS was physical proximity, so we made sure that our early morning training runs headed in the direction of TAS, even if we couldn't quite get to their gates. In return, bike riders from TAS would cycle past our buildings. We did enjoy ballroom dancing lessons with the boys in the winter term and for these we were allowed to wear ordinary clothes. This posed a dilemma for me as I had very few. Mrs Shoesmith, an amateur seamstress in Taree, came to the rescue making me a flared woollen skirt in brown checks which, despite a rather haphazard cut, looked very 'with it'. Coupled with a lovely green bolero (a short fitted cardigan) donated by Mutti (Mum) and a white school blouse, it did the trick. Other than this we had contact with the boys at mid-term and end of year dances.

We also supported TAS by the Seniors attending the annual Rugby matches with other GPS schools who came up from Sydney, as did NEGS of course. I can still remember the physical and emotional thrills all this provided; hormones buzzing, but very much under control. For the formal dances many girls ordered their ankle length ball gowns from the David Jones catalogue and there was always the chance that another girl would finish up with the same dress; a fate to be dreaded. I suspect that most of the dresses were homemade or sewn by a seamstress like our Mrs Shoesmith, who faithfully copied my designs and used the material Mutti and I bought at Rockmans in Taree.

I acquired my first boyfriend at my first dance with some misgivings. Jim Best was probably 16, quite good looking but rather shy and not sporty. I was pleased to have a boyfriend as most of my classmates didn't but I found it embarrassing to dance cheek to cheek with him. I guess I wasn't really committed. We could not see each other out of school;

boarders only left the premises on supervised trips to the dentist or for emergency shopping, nor could we talk on the phone. So we wrote letters.

I still have a little bundle somewhere that I tied with black tape (rather consciously dramatic!) after I wrote my 'Dear John' letter at the beginning of 5th Year. I did feel rather bad about that, but he looked so pathetic waiting for me in the rain, water streaming off his school hat, when I met up with him after delivering my school charges to the dentist (I was a prefect by then) that I just couldn't keep going.

Rumours were rife as to what Jim had done to deserve such a fate, none of which was true. I was told he threw my letters on the ground and stamped on them in anger, which was impressive or pathetic? What he did do at the next PLC/TAS debate, both of us were 'whip' for our teams, was to weave vague references to lampshades made of human skin into his reply to my summing up. We won and I declined to take offence, that being beneath me. The reference to Nazi atrocities was also too obscure for most of the audience to have picked up.

The next dance I was free to fill my dance card with the most eligible boys, including 'Crash' Carew, who was definitely hot. Dancing the last dance, traditionally lights out, swaying cheek to cheek with him was bliss. Not long after that Rex? won my heart. He did make a great Mikado in the school production in the Town Hall although he lacked a little height. We really enjoyed our friendship and the occasional chaste kiss. It was great to meet him for waffles and ice cream whenever I did escort duty to the dentist. Come to think of it, the boys had a lot more freedom to go into town than we did. We saw each other once in Sydney in '53 and that was rather sad as I had already met Ian by then and had to tell him so. Rex went jackarooing and died young, apparently of a weak heart.

When it came to sexual interest, one of the girls in in our dorm was a bit ahead of the rest of us. She offered to demonstrate French kissing ('yuck!') and read the first few chapters of *Love Me Sailor*, a raunchy tale of a small ship at sea with six sailors and one female cook on board, this after lights out using a torch. It was really disgusting even to her, so we returned it to TAS where it had come from still in its brown paper cover.

Later on we discovered that for one of the readings we had a young constable hiding in the garden under our open veranda dorm waiting to catch a prowler. We thought this was very funny and speculated about his opinion of our 'ladies' college.

Another very special experience for me was the Leaving Certificate. As mentioned earlier, coming to Armidale and going to boarding school saved me from educational disaster. At PLC I had a fresh start. For one, it was not possible to do the Intermediate Certificate (3rd Year) without going back two years, so going forward was the only reasonable option. I therefore started the last two years of high school (4th and 5th Years) at least a year younger than my classmates and with too big a gap to bridge in maths and the sciences to continue with these.

Fortunately I could get away with the one soft science offered at PLC, namely Physiology, and still matriculate (be eligible for university). To help finance further studies in Sydney I needed to get a Commonwealth Scholarship based on my Leaving Certificate results. So once I got the hang of the language the race was on. For me the pressure really started in 5th Year and I must say I enjoyed the challenge, loved the subjects I did and found them easy. This was fortunate for the quality of teaching varied considerably as I'll now explain.

We loved having our young sports mistress for Geography in 4th Year. The fact that she'd only got a B in the Leaving in that subject amused us. When the weather was good we persuaded her to take us out onto the back lawn for the usual 'dictation' from her own school notes. We copied these lying on our tummies (new word!) until someone ran out of ink in her fountain pen. That was the signal for us to ask questions about her boyfriend and other related topics and generally enjoy playing 'hooky' together. We were fortunate indeed that Mrs Thorpe, whose husband moved onto the faculty at UNE, arrived to put the fear of God into us in Geography for our final year.

Mrs Thorpe was inspirational, outclassing all our teachers in knowledge and wit. One of the main things I learnt from her was to use the facts we learnt to shape the answers to exam questions. Teaching at that time was mostly rote learning and the number of resources we had access to was unbelievably limited. In Modern History, for instance, we only had one text book by Roberts, which I virtually learnt by heart. What I lacked in the maths side of Geography I compensated for by creating my own combinations of maps to indicate agricultural production in various parts of the globe, among other things, during the Honours exam. My preparation had been careful practice of the outlines of continents and countries with sufficiently wiggly lines to be filled in to suit.

Mrs Thorpe was tall and elegant and due to skin problems wore no stockings, unheard of in 1952. She and her husband called in on our family in Laurieton, which was a great joy to me. No doubt they were interested to meet a successful migrant family and she to kick off her shoes so she could dabble her toes in the waves, an annual ritual apparently. I really regretted being too shy and socially incompetent to keep in touch with her and share my continuing academic success, as well as to thank her for her considerable help that year.

Our History teacher was the opposite, dull and boring for my favourite subjects, Modern and Ancient History. She had a barrel figure and wore the same brown dress day after day. She also had BO which marked her down in our books.

Our English teacher, I rather liked, but she obviously had an alcohol problem which worsened as our 5th Year wore on. She was pretty good in the morning but not with it enough to be useful after lunch, so the more ambitious classmates and I decided we would have to get ourselves exam ready on our own.

I remember Judith McLean, our head prefect who later became a psychologist, and I testing each other on possible exam questions, *Richard II* in particular. My highest mark in the Leaving was in English, not German, despite my first class honours in that language.

The elocution teacher was coerced into teaching us Physiology. She was a gentle person who did her best but reportedly had not passed the Leaving Certificate herself. We had fun dissecting and drawing sheep's hearts she got from the butcher but missed out on covering a whole section of knowledge needed for the final exam. I literally learnt everything she gave us by heart but was stumped when I discovered that gap and finished up with my only B, which I was rather cross about.

Other teachers came and went, a number of them part-time locals. It would have been hard for a small country school with a limited budget to attract good staff but The Board did its best and most of the girls there were not headed for university. For some the local Teachers' College was the answer, as was nursing training.

So now to tell you how I prepared for the exams.

In short, last minute cramming, just before and particularly during the exams, helped by NoDoze (wake up) tablets. Unbelievably I walked into the chemist in downtown Armidale in full school uniform and bought five NoDoze tablets to get me through the Leaving! I set my alarm for 3.00 am (we had to stop studying at 9.00 pm and go to bed), took my tablet, got up, rolled up my bedding (Kapok mattress etc), tiptoed past the Headmistress's bedroom to the bathrooms. There I put a shower cap over the shower head above one of the baths to catch any drips, unrolled the bedding in the tub and settled in to revise my notes for the next exam. We were allowed up at 6.00 am during the exams so I got up at 5.30 am to be on the safe side, tiptoed back, got dressed and continued my studies in the classroom at 6.00 am, breakfast and then to the High School for the exam at 9.00 am, if it were a morning session. All exams lasted three hours and sometimes there was another in the afternoon. Needless to say, not all of that information stayed in my brain after the exam was over, but then I did not need it for later in life. So there I was doing Honours in German (without a German teacher, just translating old Leaving papers back to 1927!).

We had a final fabulous dance with TAS when it was all over, six of us staying overnight at Tatts Hotel in town. Not that we used the beds much as we finished up driving through the schools, including NEGS and around the town until 5.00 am with a group of boys who had dressed in our uniforms. No 'Schoolies Week' in those days but we had our fun and recorded it on our Brownie cameras

I vividly remember the day the results of the Leaving were published in *The Sydney Morning Herald*. No advanced notice, no privacy, just page after page of results in a special supplement of the broadsheet, which in our case was not delivered so I had to collect it from Laurieton Newsagency when it arrived. The walk along the main street of

Laurieton in the glaring December sunshine seemed endless, my heart pounding with anxiety (so much for confidence). I always felt conspicuous anyway walking past those houses where I'm sure curtains twitched whenever there was movement in the quiet street. This day was worse. And then the paper. Where to start looking? Certainly not in the first 100. When I could not find my name under B for Braunschweig in the alphabetical list I had a moment of real anxiety; then I found it, equal 64th in the State. What a buzz! I flew back along that street. hanging onto the bulky paper, suffused with gratitude and joy. What a way to say thank you to my parents for their sacrifice, their trust in me. There I was with First Class Honours in German, Second Class Honours in Geography, A grade in English, Modern History and Ancient History, and a B in Physiology. As I said, I found out about my better result in English than German at a later interview.

My choice of career was limited to a BA at Sydney University with little prospect other than teaching, or Occupational Therapy (O.T.), which was only a diploma course at the time (as was Physiotherapy). I had had totally unrealistic dreams of medicine and was good with my hands, so my parents thought that O.T. with its combination of medical subjects and craftwork would be ideal. My Commonwealth Scholarship would cover the fees at the O.T. College which operated under the aegis of Sydney University.

Unfortunately my parents had to fund the text books and living expenses as by then their combined income was too high, but that fortunately was manageable.

Although I attended PLC Armidale as a boarder for only two years (1950/51) it made an incredible contribution to my life and I still have very clear recollections of that time, far more than I have written down. I think there are only two of us left from my year and we are still in touch each Christmas.

Toni Playford (née Yates) 1953-1955

I was at PLC Armidale for Years Two, Three and Four. The Headmistresses were Miss Kathleen Buchan and then Miss Jean McColl. Main House became my 'home away from home' for three years. I am one of the Birida Bunch. There my character developed, from ages 13 to 16. It was a holistic experience that remained with me for the rest of my life. I was privileged and thankful for that experience and opportunity.

My appreciation has been for my lifelong friends from those years. We are now 80-year-olds, living interstate from each other, but still in contact.

Heather Bardsley (Briggs Davie) with her mother, and me with mine, were the first to arrive at the dormitory selected for us. Introductions then conversations continued until our mothers left. Our friendship continued. Later we were each other's bridesmaids. We call ourselves sisters.

Jennifer (Jenny) Johnson (Burnett) came to PLC in 1954 and her sister, Dinah, a year ahead of me at PLC, asked me to look after her. In 1955 Jenny and I were in the same dorm and became lifelong friends.

Denise Bernard (Imerson), although a boarder in Junior House, became a close school friend. On leaving PLC our paths ultimately diverged and we lost contact. My husband, Tom said he could find her and within 15 minutes he had located her husband's brother! We happily reconnected and stay in touch.

Gwen Rowe (Carless), like me came from Manilla, NSW. Our families were friends and Gwennie and I had been close friends as small children. We were 'bosom pals'…apologies to L.M. Montgomery's *Anne of Green Gables*. We remained close until she died in 2012.

I grew in independence, being away from home and having to stand on my own two feet.

My Christian faith was fostered at PLC. I came from a family that regularly worshipped at a Presbyterian church, so they wished me to attend PLC as a natural progression of my growing and maturing. We had Assembly five days each week, beginning with a devotion, a Bible reading, a prayer from a mistress and a hymn accompanied by one of the students on the piano. Often it was my friend Gwennie. Evening devotion was again in the Assembly Hall. On Sunday morning the school walked in an orderly line to the Presbyterian Church, occasionally to the Methodist or Church of England, widening our worship experience. And in our elocution classes we used passages of scripture - Psalm 23, Isiah 53 etc.

I found my niche in physical exercises termed 'Drill' and performed regularly to music as a group. 'Drill Bar' was an annual event held on the front lawn of *Birida*.

A badge was given to the winner of the 'Drill Bar' competition in each year group, judged by a visiting judge. That year there was a tie for our year between Irmgard Brunswick and myself. Because they didn't have two badges neither of us received one! I was a bit disappointed. I had tennis coaching at that time and continued to play socially post PLC. I have continued throughout my life with physical exercise and tennis, playing golf as well; today I do 'Essential Physiotherapy'. I also find swimming a good exercise as I did at PLC.

My love for music taught me to commit to practice and to appreciate my teacher, Miss Joyce Adams and her patience. Miss Adams would come to the dormitory at 6.00 am to wake me for my piano practice. She disturbed the rest of the dormitory at the same time. She must have risen early, walking from the teachers' residence across the road. My mother had knitted a pair of bottle green mittens which I could use for practice on cold winter mornings. Eventually I rebelled. Our dorm was on a verandah enclosed by a lattice mesh between us and the elements, so was freezing cold. (This kind of accommodation was not unusual in those days). Miss Adams came to the dormitory, called my name (my bed was at the far end of the dormitory), I pulled the bedclothes over my head, she stamped her foot and left. Another practice time was introduced. Miss Adams took me to my final music examinations before I left PLC; Grade 5 with Honours. The examiner for this exam was the composer of one of the pieces that I played. It was an unforgettable experience.

[Ed. The examiner would have been Miriam Hyde.]

Remembering the 'Tuck Box Shed' brings me smiles; a food source brought from home! The shed stood in the grounds just below the tennis courts. It was an octagonal lattice construction and had one entrance with a locked door. It was a provision of extra food for the Main House students, the boarders. Inside, shelves around the walls accommodated the treasured 'tuck boxes'. The boxes were usually bulk biscuit tins locked for protection! I'm sure we would have trusted each other, so it must have been from mice or ants maybe? They were filled with treats from home, prepared lovingly at the end of the holidays. Cakes, biscuits, slices savoury and sweet. Fruit cake especially was a good lasting source as these provisions had to last the term! Recipes were often shared to take back home, for example:

CHEESE BUTTONS

Ingredients:
3oz plain flour
2oz butter
3oz grated cheese
1 tbsp. water
good pinch cayenne
1 tspn. lemon juice
celery salt and grated cheese to sprinkle on top

Method:
Sift flour, salt and cayenne, rub butter in lightly, add cheese.
Mix to dry dough with water and lemon juice.
Use more water if necessary.
Roll out thinly, cut into small rounds, glaze with milk, sprinkle with celery salt and cheese.
Bake on greased tray, hot oven, about 19 minutes.

The green grocer sold fruit to PLC students. I was a customer and, with permission, stored half a case of Granny Smith apples in my port in 'The Loft' above the music rooms. Probably the apples lasted all term. I still love the taste of Granny Smiths!

The meals were good at PLC and no one went hungry. We sat at tables formally with a prefect seated with us teaching us table manners. For an after school snack we queued for a piece of fresh bread and jam (no butter) or a piece of fruit. These always went down well.

Apart from the end-of-year formal dance for the older year group we were not encouraged to have any contact with the opposite, well, BOYS. I was however acquainted with Teddy Copeland who had been in the same class as me at Manilla Primary School and who was now at TAS. He used to send me a letter in Fourth Year, dropping it in the PLC letterbox. I used to look out for it and run and collect it. It was a platonic friendship which I remember fondly.

Betty Parsons and I were permitted to leave the school grounds to attend Technical College drafting lessons, a privilege. One day Teddy was cycling past with a friend and stopped to say, 'Hello'. By sheer chance Miss Davies saw us talking to boys in the street. We were called to the front of the whole school before dinner that night and held up as a disgrace to the school and an example of bad behaviour. I still remember the humiliation of that reprimand. It could have been dealt with privately. Ted accompanied me to the end of year ball at The Armidale Tennis Club House. I would like to see him again and introduce him to my family and meet his also.

PLC was very conscious of the fact that the girls attending when I did were from the background of World War II. My father was absent those years as were many others. For some there had been difficulty and hardship. Money was in short supply for some families and thus, to some degree for the school. Recently drought, bushfires and COVID-19 have threatened our stability and comfort. The care, as well as the education, at PLC enabled me to leave the school with personal stability, confidence and my head held high. For all this I am very appreciative.

Leaving school I became a nurse, married, had three children and now have eight grandchildren and three great-grandchildren. I nursed in country hospitals, worked in residential care and volunteered in a hostel near my home town of Lobethal, SA before retiring.

With my dear husband Tom who has been commissioned by The Uniting Church, we work in the Mount Torrens Uniting Church in the Adelaide Hills. We share our house with a family, victims of the 20/12/2019 Cudlee Creek bushfire.

Church for the Mount Torrens members since COVID-19 has meant meeting in our home while following the restrictions of social distancing and the rules of hand sanitising. Plans are in place for us to return to the church building before Christmas.

I believe in respecting the values and beliefs of others, in giving and sharing. I learned from my years at PLC that happiness comes from that.

Beth McKee tells of her sister's experience in 1953

My sister Heather Clyne tells the story of how in 1953 a prowler got into the 3rd Year South Dorm, took the dressing gown off her bed and got into bed with Heather Parsons.

When she screamed he took off.

They must have caught him because Heather remembers going to court and her dressing gown mentioned as evidence.

Barbara McHattan (née Reid) 1950-1958

In my time at PLC I experienced all three boarding houses, Prep, Junior and Main.

I remember my Primary teacher, Miss Evelyn Moffatt, as being a very kind teacher to a lonely, scared little girl. She gave me an award for reading (1952) and spelling (1953) which I believe engendered a lifelong passion for reading.

High School teacher, Mrs Gwen Kelly was inspirational and was able to make History come to life. I enjoyed reading her book, *Middle Aged Maidens*. Was it about us? Miss Cooper was the Science teacher. Miss M. Joyce Adams was my Music teacher and without her never ending encouragement and high heels tapping to get me out of bed for early morning practice I would never have made the grade.

How could I ever forget out Headmistress, Miss J. McColl telling me I had no hope of getting into nursing. How I would love to tell her that I did and only retired early in 2020, so there!

We had performances of Gilbert and Sullivan, *Iolanthe* and *Pirates of Penzance* in the Town Hall. I was in the chorus—all good fun.

Dormitory life was always cold. I still cannot sleep well in a heated room. Hair wash happened on Saturdays and we'd dry it out in the sun. Junior House had only a bath.

I remember only one excursion and that was to the Uralla Lagoon for Biology.

For church every Sunday we walked there in a crocodile formation. Being there taught me to sit still and take my mind elsewhere. This has been useful in yoga practice in later years.

PLC provided a very sheltered environment consisting of all women and was very protected.

Annabelle Sinclair 1949-1956

Memories of my year at boarding school; 1953.

I was 11 and became a weekly boarder at Prep House because my parents were preparing to sell our property at Moree. Previously I had been a day girl from 1949 and was again a day girl after this year up until 1956 when I left PLC and attended Presbyterian Girl's College (PGC) Warwick in Queensland.

Being a weekly boarder meant that sometimes my mother took me home to our house in Armidale or I went to stay at the homes of family friends who were neighbours in Armidale. There were also weekends when I stayed at Prep House with all the full time boarders.

Miss Hutton was in charge of the boarding house. I remember her being a kind person and she must have been tolerant to deal with a house full of pre-teen and teenage girls and even younger ones.

I shared a room with two other girls across the hall from Miss Hutton's room. I remember reading under the sheets with a torch and eating peanut butter. Tuck boxes were popular and were stocked with fruit cake and biscuits from our mothers, also vegemite and peanut butter. They were kept by the house mistress.

A historic event was celebrated as we sat in Miss Hutton's sitting room and listened to the broadcast of the coronation of the present queen in 1953.

I have a memory of there being a 'prowler' reported at night in the grounds round Prep house. The screaming and panic that ensued was quite deafening but we were all shepherded into a group and calmed down by our House mistress and an on-duty policeman. No one was apprehended.

Other events I remember were Sunday nights when we wore black velvet dresses with white lace collars in the presence of the Headmistress Miss Ashworth at Main House. No recollection of what the point was though. Weekends dragged a bit but we sat in the sun on our rugs on the lawn in the Prep House garden in groups, reading and sunbaking.

A whole school picnic was sometimes organised and we would enjoy a trip to Commissioner's Waters and cool off in the creek on a hot summery day.

Food doesn't figure prominently in my memory of that year. Just queueing up for fresh white bread, butter and plum jam out of rather large tins which, I think, was a snack after school and before midday dinner.

Sadly I had many traumatic experiences with a temporary teacher of mathematics, who proceeded to humiliate me in class. Her teaching methods left much to be desired and I am sure she would have been reported in today's world. Hitting me with a ruler and leaning over me as I worked, made certain that I was terrified of her and almost always got the answer wrong. No one has ever been more grateful than me that calculators were invented!

Walking down to church on Sundays in a crocodile formation is a strong memory. The high volume sermons of hellfire and brimstone delivered by Reverend Saunders accompanied by banging on the pulpit were sometimes a highlight. The ladies of the congregation in their hats and gloves and the great importance paid to the state of our own school uniforms before appearing in public is a strong memory.

Heather Bardsley (née Briggs Davie) 1953-1955

OUR 2nd YEAR CLASS

A is for Agnes who has lovely hair,
B is for Betty who's dark not fair,
C is for Caroline one with the brains,
D is for Denise her book has no stains,
E is for Elspeth the brainiest by far,
F is for Fay the tennis star,
H is for Helen who does her work well.
I is for Irmgard whose English fell,
J is for Judith the lover of drawing,
M is for Maggie finds algebra boring,
P is for Pam who had a bad fall,
R is for Robyn so very small,
S is for Suzanne who invented 'to bop',
T is for Truda and here I will stop.

Heather aged 12 years.

Heather Benning (née Noon) 1950-1958

I attended PLC as a boarder from 1950 to 1958. I first started off at Prep House which faced Faulkner Street and Miss Hutton was the House Mistress. Some of us were quite young, 7, 8 and 9 years old. After a few years at Prep House I moved to Junior House in Brown Street near the classroom block. I think Miss Williams was there for a while and was better known as 'Willy'. She expected very good discipline at all times and made us do everything correctly in the Dining Room including getting around with a ruler if we did not sit up straight. From Junior House I moved to *Birida* which was called Main House. Miss Ashworth was the Principal when I first started school followed by Miss Buchan and then Miss McColl. Muriel Davies was Deputy Principal and some of the teachers lived in a nearby house in Marsh Street.

When I first started at school the dining room was in *Birida* and a new dining room was built behind *Birida* and next to the School Hospital which Sister Mears ran. If you had a cold you were given white medicine or black cough mixture or perhaps an aspro.

Food was not the best; stew, hash and porridge in particular, but we all survived. Morning and afternoon teas were brown bread with quince jam or melon and lemon jam. When I first started, school dinner at night was a black velvet dress and black patent shoes occasion.

We used to have cocoa with watered down milk and Elva was a kitchen staff member who was kind to all of us. Baked dinners on a Sunday were the best. As time marched on we were allowed to have tuck boxes in a shed near the tennis courts where we had cakes, biscuits and fruit. Abood Brothers Fruit Shop delivered us a bag of fruit once a week which our parents paid for.

Each Sunday we went to the Tuck Shop and bought one shillings worth of sweets which was pretty exciting in those days. Most Sunday afternoons we spent walking around Armidale. We had Assembly every morning and evening and went to St Paul's Presbyterian church every Sunday morning. We had white dresses with green bows for church and special occasions and always wore hats and gloves. Speech Day was an especially big occasion and was held in the Town Hall. We used to have movies each Saturday night in the room where we had Assemblies. We occasionally went to the pictures for something special or to ABC concerts at the Town Hall.

Mid-term was always nice as you went home and took friends with you. I played tennis and basketball (netball) and if you were a swimmer you walked to and from the public baths before breakfast for training. We would go for picnics at the Pine Forest, Commissioner's Waters or Rocky River by bus.

I think my days at PLC were very rewarding. I made many friends and we are all still in contact. When I think back the food was very basic, the accommodation not the best, but we all survived.

Margaret Davidson (née Brett) 1949-1953

I was a day girl until 1952 and a boarder only in 1953. We day girls used to eat lunch in a designated area in the grounds in fine weather and as a boarder we would 'study?' for the Leaving Certificate in the grounds of Prep House up near the tennis courts.

PLC joined the town march in 1953 celebrating the coronation of Queen Elizabeth II. The banner became very heavy by the end of the journey.

As a boarder for such a short time my tales of strange and surprising incidents are very few and I'm sure the boarders would have some lovely tales to tell.

The new dining room and kitchen were opened in our time and, although new, it was most unhygienic and unattractive. I do remember finding maggots in the cold meat salad that was served up for tea one night. Luckily that only happened once.

I remember poor old 'Willy' or 'Wild Willy Whiskers' who struggled to keep control of Junior House.

One day of the week, after morning break we used to have a maths 'lesson?' in the spare room between the gym and the music rooms, labelled a 'free period'. We were supposed to do maths work between two maths periods. This room had a fireplace and being winter we actually had a fire. Dorothy Jardine, known as 'Sardine', came up with the idea she could hop over to the potato store and bring back some potatoes to cook in the coals. This she did and was busy telling all how Willy nearly caught her when a voice at the door said, 'Willy nearly did, did she?' As you can imagine, dead silence, confiscation of the potatoes and a detention for Sardine.

Summer time, come Friday, the swimmers all marched down to the local baths for a few lessons, but mainly for fun. I think we must have had inter-school carnivals but don't remember much about them. We walked everywhere; no one thought of buses.

The only excursion I remember was in 1953 when our lovely Geography teacher, Mrs Thorpe planned a bus trip from Armidale to the mid north coast. Great excitement as we were also to be accompanied by Miss Shirley Purkiss, secretary to Miss Buchan our Headmistress, both great travelling companions. So, of course, I got shingles in my eye just before departure and broken hearted was returned home to my mother.

A great time was had by all.

Janet Witham (née Weatherburn) 1954-1956

Sixty five years is a lifetime ago and yet for me there are so many memories of that time, a time of saying farewell to childhood and crossing the threshold of adulthood, learning to stand on my own two feet, and being more responsible for my actions. However life was not always serious. In fact I remember those three years as being full of friendship, fun and filled with an abundance of new and exciting experiences. So, I look back on that time fondly and thank those teachers and fellow students who helped me in so many ways.

At the time that I began secondary schooling at PLC in February, 1954, my sister, Hilary, was starting her fourth year. Our parents were living at Keepit Dam on the Namoi River between Tamworth and Gunnedah. As the engineers and their families lived a couple of miles from the workmen's village I only met up with children of my own age during school hours. So, for me, the prospect of going to boarding school was a chance of making real friends for the first time.

Being a boarder was also a new experience. Sharing a bedroom with three others in Prep House, one soon developed not only friendships but also gave support to those in need. One such example was to wake one night to hear one of my roommates crying. Poor lass had discovered she was bleeding and had no idea why. Fortunately, two of us had already been 'initiated' to 'George' (as we all referred to menstruation then) and a quiet word to my sister, who then had a quiet word to the victim's sister, soon resolved the matter.

I remember very little about the Prep house matron, unlike the Junior House matron. I can't remember the name of this second lady but she was a large, tall woman who in 2nd Year gave us quite a bit of leeway.

She was firm but, in my eyes, very fair. I look back in amazement now when I recall that she allowed the four of us sharing the Blue Room, in the front of Junior House, to paint its walls! What sort of a job we did, I can't recall, and who supplied the equipment, I do not know. It wouldn't be allowed today what with the Occupational Work and Safety Act now in law. But just think; we saved the school some money by not having to pay a professional to do the job!

In my 3rd Year we moved up to the South Dorm in the Main House which had formerly been a long verandah at the back of the house. Boy, was it cold in winter! I well remember thick bed socks which I had never needed before and taking my underwear into bed at night and putting them on in the morning before rising. Fortunately, once we had breakfast (the porridge was runny and nothing like Dad cooked at home) and got out and about, we soon warmed up.

Unfortunately, I was also responsible for a bit of 'demolition' in my year in Main House, for which I presume my parents had to pay. On the first occasion, I leant back on a hand basin and the bowl fell to the floor. I claimed that the basin had a crack in it but had to admit fault on the 2nd occasion when I broke the shower-rose over one of the baths. I was standing on the edge of the bath (for what reason I know not) when I over-balanced and grabbed the shower arm to save my fall. I'm not surprised it broke; I was no lightweight.

I was not really fond of any of the meals; nothing tasted as good as the food my mother cooked. However, there might have been another reason why I didn't look forward to meal times. I had always been a slow eater and this did not go down well with those at my table. One of the senior girls always sat at the top of the table, then by class we sat along the sides of the table with the most junior at the other end. That was where I sat during my first year. No one was allowed to leave the table until everyone had finished eating which meant that in first year, in particular, I got many withering looks at my slow pace. If the atmosphere got really bad, I would bolt the last of my food, a habit of which I am still guilty.

One cannot record memories of those years without making reference to life in the classroom. After all, learning and broadening our knowledge of subjects which would or could be useful in the future was the reason our parents had sent us to PLC Armidale. One aspect, to which I had to get used in my first few months, was that there was only one class in the room and we had separate teachers for each subject. My primary schooling had been at a two-teacher school where learning was very different and could often be very distracting.

School work was always going to be a challenge for me as subjects like science, maths (particularly algebra and trigonometry), Latin and French held little interest for me. My favourite subjects were all to do with expression – history, writing (particularly poetry), art, music and anything creative. How happy I was when I had the opportunity to learn weaving, a craft I did for many years. After moving to Melbourne in 1972 with a young family, I began teaching night classes in weaving at a local Technical College.

I have very happy memories of the loft over the music rooms either attending art classes or designing, threading up a loom and watching the pattern growing as I sat there weaving. In fact, that whole building (I was once told that it had been the stables for *Birida*) held happy memories for me. The music rooms were below the loft and it was in one or another of them that I spent many hours after school practising, instead of playing sport. (Any excuse to get out of sport!).

In front of the music rooms was a small hall where we learnt ballroom dancing and also put on other entertainment. I'm sure my love of music, singing and the theatre was certainly enhanced greatly by the opportunities offered at PLC.

And there were plenty of opportunities to enjoy those arts. My music lessons with Miss Wharton across the way in Marsh Street were always a joy. Singing in church, in morning assembly, in the choir, school events and attending concerts put on annually by the Sydney Symphony Orchestra were highlights in my three years in Armidale. However, my most vivid memory is the school performance of *Iolanthe* in the Armidale Town Hall at the end of my final year. I played (and sang) the role of Lord Tolloller and, if my memory serves me well, Christine Ewing was Lord Mountararat. What a ball we had and to top it off my mother arrived in time to see the show. I had no idea she was coming but I was informed during the interval. What a thrill!

Growing up in the country, I had the opportunity to be adventurous and develop an interest in nature. Boarding school gave me the opportunity to have more of those experiences during mid-term breaks. I was very fortunate to have friends who would invite me to stay with them on such occasions as my home was too far away and transport too difficult for such a short time. Robyn McGufficke's, Libby Manuel's and Diana Lindsay's families all lived on properties with plenty to do and see, places to explore, and be well fed.

Sport, as I have mentioned before, was not an activity I enjoyed, probably because I was no sprinter or at all agile. Running in the morning had no appeal whatsoever. However, I did enjoy eurhythmics (probably because it was to music) and the impromptu evening walks. I also enjoyed the many opportunities we had swimming but I didn't excel in that either. It wasn't until years later when I first experienced skiing that I found a sport to enjoy with balance being an attribute with which I had been blessed.

I don't remember names of many of my teachers but I do remember Miss Davies. She taught art amongst other subjects and also accompanied those of us travelling south on the train for holiday breaks. Talking of train trips, one time travelling home, the New Zealand All Blacks team was also on board having been in Armidale to play Rugby. They were a very friendly bunch and spent much of the journey singing. They then asked us to sing Waltzing Matilda, for which we made a very self-conscious effort. They then sang it with us but we soon stopped and let them carry on as their voices and harmony were so good.

Miss Buchan was Headmistress for my first two years and Miss McColl followed her. I vividly remember Miss McColl for she wore bright red framed glasses and I had never seen any coloured framed glasses before. Soon after the start of the year, she called me over as we left assembly and my first reaction was that I had done something wrong. But no, she asked me if I were any relation to Professor C.E. Weatherburn, the mathematician at the University of Western Australia. Miss McColl had apparently studied a number of his books at university.

When I replied that he was my grandfather, her eyes lit up as I think she imagined that she had a budding mathematician in her school. How I must have disappointed her when I only achieved a Pass in maths for my Intermediate Certificate!

I'm sure I could remember more of my years at PLC Armidale if I really tried but I feel I have covered most activities and impressions. My last two years of Secondary School were spent at PLC Croydon, now known as PLC Sydney. In early 1957 my father was transferred to the W.C. & I.C. head office in Sydney and with Hilary then at Sydney University, my parents felt that it would be best if we were all, more or less, together again.

It is hard for me to pinpoint what influences PLC had on my future life but I'm sure there was much I gained from the opportunities, encouragement and support I was given by so many people. I trained as a nurse at RPA and did my Midwifery training in Canberra, a profession which stood me in good stead when my husband, David, and our three children moved to Halls Gap in the Victorian Grampians in 1977. David, who was the Director of the Outward Bound school on the Hawkesbury River when I met him, was keen to set up an outdoor education business of his own and I could not think of a better place than 'back in the bush' to bring up our family. So while David built our house, I returned to nursing as the Senior Night Sister at Stawell Hospital for five years and another five years on weekend day duty.

All the things I relished at PLC are still part of my life. Researching and writing about local history, giving PowerPoint presentations on that subject and also on my world travels: Zimbabwe and Kenya, Hong Kong and Mongolia, the Trans-Siberian railway, Moscow and St. Petersburg, Argentina and Antarctica, to name a few; my love of Nature, which I have the joy (and distraction) of witnessing out of my kitchen window every day – kangaroos, wallabies, echidnas, emu and so many other bush birds; needlework in its many forms and music which is still so important to me.

Oh, how I have missed my six annual visits to hear the Melbourne Symphony Orchestra this year because of the Covid virus! At least I have been given piano 'recitals' by my grandchildren whenever I visit. They are a great joy to me (and good at maths!).

So, all in all, I look back on my years at PLC Armidale in Brown Street with great affection and I am sure our inspiring school motto, *Ad Astra*, had a lot to do with my enjoyment and achievements during the rest of my life.

Beth McKee (née Clyne) 1954-1958

When I was in Junior House I decided to see if it was possible to fit through the bars of the window. I got to the top and as a joke one of the girls cried, 'Here comes Willie' and I leapt down onto the nearest bed and it broke.

I asked Willie to sign my year book at the end of the year and she wrote, 'To the heavy weight of Junior House.'

Patricia Harrison 1950-1956

My family lived in Armidale, so for most of my seven years at PLC, I was one of a very small group of day girls. However, I was a weekly boarder for part of my final year, while preparing for the Leaving Certificate, as the HSC was called back then, and for years I regularly had morning tea and hot lunches at school with the boarders. Also, since most of my school friends were boarders, I picked up a lot of information about their school lives over the years. All of my PLC years were spent in the old premises in Brown St.

Some general impressions that stand out most in my memory are these:

First, that although boarders often complained, I think most were reasonably happy with life at PLC. We made good friends and enjoyed doing things together.

The majority of our boarders came from farms and small communities in Northern NSW. Access to secondary schooling near their homes was limited. One family were post-war migrants from Europe and another girl's parents ran a tea plantation in India. This I found fascinating, but students with international backgrounds were rare. Like most of Australia at the time, we were a pretty monochrome, monocultural bunch!

I occasionally holidayed at the homes of a couple of my boarder friends and greatly enjoyed the experiences. I'm convinced that living away from home intensified most boarders' devotion to their homes and parents (and often to their horses too). Going home for the holidays was eagerly anticipated. Day girls probably took their homes and families more for granted.

The expectations of students, families and the wider community were very different in post-war days to those that apply now. Take, for instance, my following more specific recollections. A couple of these might be reported in the tabloids or give rise to enquiries were they to occur in a contemporary Australian boarding school. At least parents would have something to say. But we simply accepted such things, shrugged our shoulders, complained a bit, then just got on with life. I think our families' memories of both wartime restrictions and the ravages of the Spanish Flu and the Depression kept small inconveniences in perspective.

Some specific memories include:

Morning tea normally consisted of a hunk of bread with jam and no butter, plus cocoa with no milk. (The warm drink was appreciated in Armidale winters.)

The midday meal was the main one each day and was usually quite a healthy traditional Australian meat and veg dish. Dessert was often sago or tapioca, frequently topped with burnt flakes. (The cooks evidently had difficulty getting that right.)

The evening meal, especially on weekends, was often a bit inadequate for growing teenagers. I remember, for instance, that this would quite often consist of one boiled egg, after which we could fill up with bread and spread.

Armidale weather could be a bit challenging, and heating was not always adequate. I remember sometimes taking a hot water bag to class. At one stage a few of us had to sleep on a fairly open verandah with blinds but no windows. (There were rumours of a man having climbed onto that verandah one night, though little was said about that.)

Hygiene was not the best. I remember wearing thongs in the shower because there were sometimes worms wriggling around the floor drain! And once I found a dead rat, apparently partly eaten by a cat, under my pillow!

Academic standards were not great in my first couple of years, in contrast with my earlier years in a state primary school. I don't believe teachers were required to have teacher training then, just a qualification in some content area. At PLC we had a nice teacher in our combined 5th and 6th classes. But she did spend a rather a lot of time reading stories to us, and we also spent quite a few afternoons gardening and pulling weeds.

Somewhat surprisingly, given the view of women's role at the time, PLC had no Domestic Science courses other than Dressmaking. Perhaps less surprisingly, when I first went there, it had no Science lab. The only sciences offered were Physiology and Geography.

However, all that changed under a new principal as I advanced into high school. PLC added Science courses, a lab and a good teacher. Students could then take Physics and Chemistry to Leaving Certificate standard. (This came a bit late for me.) Thanks to the University, we were able to recruit some well-qualified teachers with international experience. Some were wives of UNE lecturers, or part-time lecturers themselves. During my final years at PLC our small classes and good teachers provided a learning experience second to none. We had excellent teachers for some of my favourite subjects, including English, French, Geography and Ancient and Modern History. I did well in my Leaving Certificate and am very thankful for those years.

I have always had a strong interest in languages, but in the 1950s, most language instruction centred on grammar and written work, with little attention to oral communication. At PLC we gained a solid background in French grammar, reading and writing, but I needed private tutoring with a French national to work more on speaking and listening. During my years at PLC I was also teaching myself German. I was able to practise this language with a school friend, Gerlinde, from an Austrian family. We both wanted to take German for the Leaving Certificate and the school was able to procure us a German tutor just for several months in our final year of school. This was much appreciated and was enough help for us to sit the exam and do well.

I do not recall any school excursions, and extracurricular activities were limited.

Over several years I studied piano with a teacher related to me who lived just around the corner in Marsh Street. During free periods twice a week I would go to her home for music lessons. I never became much of a pianist, mainly due to lack of ongoing practice, but I valued learning the basics. I later taught myself to play even more basic Hawaiian guitar and ukulele.

I was never well coordinated, so my attempts at ballroom dancing and at all team sports were disastrous. Our Phys. Ed. teacher had little patience with my poor coordination and to me, PE lessons always had a somewhat militaristic feel! Dancing lessons and tennis coaching were frustrating experiences that got me nowhere. But non-competitive, individual sport was okay. I liked going to the pool but was never much of a swimmer, and I rather enjoyed roller skating round the gym.

The occasional dances PLC held with TAS were eagerly anticipated for months. PLC and NEGS competed for the attention of the TAS boys! Being in an all-girls environment made it difficult for some to relate well to boys, although I and several senior boarders had the advantage of participating in the Presbyterian Fellowship Association (youth group), and getting to know a number of boys in a normal setting rather than in the hype of a formal! That definitely made things easier when starting Uni.

I enjoyed the Arts Council and ABC concerts we were sometimes treated to in Armidale. And whether or not I participated, I greatly enjoyed the more-or-less annual Gilbert and Sullivan operettas performed by TAS, PLC (and maybe NEGS?). Some of these were combined ventures, others run by one school. Adult singers were sometimes 'borrowed' from UNE or elsewhere to play difficult main parts. I loved the year PLC did *Iolanthe*.

In answer to the question, 'How did my PLC education affect my subsequent life?' my answer is: Considerably. Especially in the area of Languages and Linguistics, which have always been one important strand in my life. My language background enabled me to enrol in an Arts degree at UNE, studying English, French and German. I graduated with Honours in German and went on to do a Dip Ed, becoming a teacher of Modern Languages, English and History. I also taught primary classes for a time, and later did an MEd in Teaching English (Adult TESOL) from the University of South Australia. I taught English to overseas students at UNE for a time, and later held my own English tutoring sessions and eventually trained ESL teachers.

My love of Gilbert and Sullivan has persisted too, although these days it is becoming harder to find live performances and I must mostly resort to recordings.

On the other hand, PLC Phys. Ed. lessons and school sports had an enduring negative impact. I hated team sports, as I felt I was always letting my team down, and when the girls nominated their own teams, I was often the last one chosen. To this day, I never attend sporting events and usually change the channel the moment anything 'sporty' appears on TV. (I realise I am missing something that most people evidently enjoy; something that would have also provided more much-needed exercise in my adult life). There are a few exceptions; I enjoy watching gymnastics, skiing and ice skating.

The way less sports-oriented kids are treated in school is important! I know others who were turned off most sport for life by unhappy school experiences. The flip side of this is that when teaching primary school, I could empathise with the kids who were not sports-oriented; I tried to help them find individual sports they could enjoy *alongside* others, rather than in competition.

A downside of attending a school that mainly catered for boarders has been that within a few years of graduating, I lost touch with most of my school friends. Hardly any lived in Armidale, so on finishing school, they vanished to the four winds – back to their homes or elsewhere for work or further education. And most married and changed their names. When I've attended Old Girls' functions, I've generally known nobody; these events understandably seem to attract more recent students.

My sister, on the other hand, attended Armidale High School, and to this day she often visits old school friends in Armidale.

Did PLC influence my religious or political views? Not really. I do not remember much study or discussion of political themes, human rights or social justice in my school years. Nothing much about women's role in society other than traditional assumptions. Little about the environment, except in Geography. Nothing about theology or world religions.

As was so often the case, the various ministers' short RE (Religious Education) lessons were not very stimulating and I suspect that compulsory church attendance turned off more girls than it inspired. However, I attended the Presbyterian church with my family, not with the school. I became quite involved with the youth group and appreciated our many thoughtful studies and discussions, alongside our social life. (It would have been good to have similar discussions in the context of our school).

I became more committed to a Christian approach to life in University and from my own reading, and that began to dovetail with my strong interest in human rights and social justice. I went on to study Theology and World Religions in the USA, and eventually completed a PhD in the Departments of Education and Studies in Religion at the University of Queensland.

My commitment to aid and development, human rights, environmental concerns, women's issues and social justice later took me to Oxford, where I completed a Master's degree in Political Ethics. My political stance has moved in the direction of my concerns about such issues.

I served for 8 years on the National Board of TEAR Australia (Transformation, Empowerment, Advocacy, Relief) an inter-church aid and development agency (now Tearfund) that works in some of the world's poorest nations.

My five years in America coincided with the Civil Rights Movement and the Women's Movement and I became involved in both.

After a few years of school teaching and overseas study, I lectured for four years at Armidale CAE (College of Advanced Education) and UNE and really enjoyed my time there. I then moved into lecturing at several theological colleges over a number of years, while also undertaking a good deal of voluntary education consultancy with churches and colleges in developing countries. I continue some of this work today.

So PLC has strongly influenced certain areas of my life; other areas not so much. But overall, I am thankful for the grounding I received there, and for the friends I made.

The new dining hall building. *Photo: Catherine Gough (née McKechnie).*

Day girls in their lunch area, 1952 - L-R Marion Kemmis, Mary Jenkins, Janice Todd, Helen Todd, Gwen McKenzie.
Photo: Margaret Davidson (née Brett).

Prefects in the Coronation celebratory town march, June 1953. Margaret Brett (with banner) - L-R Catherine Campbell, Judith Reid, Judith Arndel. *Photo: Margaret Davidson (née Brett).*

Drill Bar on the front lawn in green sport tunics with blue tassels, 1954. *Photo: Toni Playford (née Yates).*

School library, first floor school block, 1952.
Photo: Gerlinde Spencer (née Braunschweig).

Geography excursion group, 1953.
Photo: Margaret Davidson (née Brett).

Ready for the dance, 1955 - Jennifer Burnett and Toni Yates.
Photo: Toni Playford (née Yates).

1954 Prefects and Headmistress. Back L-R Margaret McDonnell, Jean Muir, J. Manning, E. McLean, C. Hunter, M. Jenkins J. Reid
Seated: L-R Marion Kemmis, Miss Jean McColl, (Headmistress), Margaret Mitchell (Head Prefect). *Photo: PLC Archives.*

1955 Prefects and Headmistress.
Back L-R Hilary Weatherburn (Head prefect), Miss Jean McColl, (Headmistress), Helen Sabine.
Front L-R Jill Beath, M. Willis, Faye Davidson, Nancye McDonald, Gwen Carliss. *Photo: PLC Archives.*

Mucking up in the dorm. *Photo: Margaret Davidson (née Brett).*

Gymnastic display on the front lawn, c. 1955. *Photo: PLC Archives.*

Mr William (Billy) McBean,
Chairman of PLC School
Council and School Dentist.
Photo: PLC Archives.

Miss Miriam Davies, Deputy
Headmistress, Art and Craft
teacher, 1953.
Photo: PLC Archives.

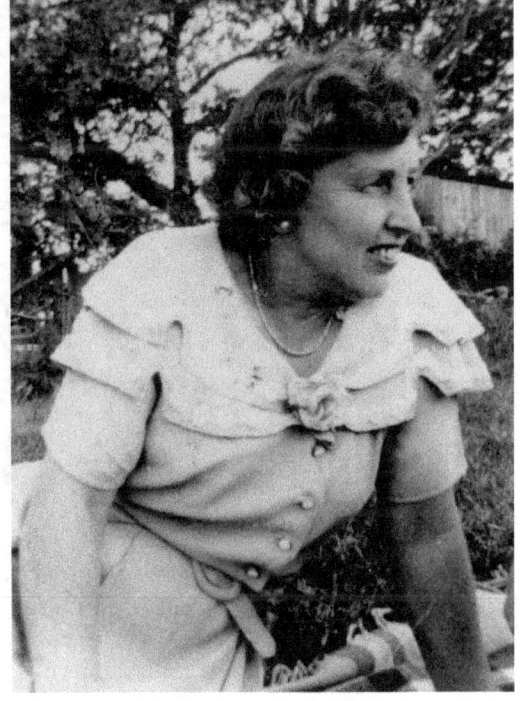

Whole school with Principal, Kathleen Buchan, 1953. *Photo: PLC Archives.*

PART THREE

The Late 1950s and Early 1960s

Introduction

The one millionth post war immigrant arrived in Australia in 1955 and six o'clock pub closing time was changed to 10 o'clock. Armidale Memorial Library moved into its own building in Faulkner Street. Once again NSW was beset by floods and at Maitland about 100 houses were swept away and over 2,000 damaged.

The 16th Olympic Games were held in Melbourne in 1956 which became an exciting year with the beginning of the era of drive-in cinemas and the first regular TV broadcasts from Channel TCN 9. The Oaky River Hydro Power Station began supplementing electricity power to Armidale.

Unfortunately in 1957 a bad epidemic broke out, known as The Asian Flu and bush fires in the Blue Mountains claimed five lives. Utzon won the prize for the best design for the proposed Opera House in Sydney and Armidale's 2AD radio station commenced broadcasting. In October of 1957 Russia successfully launched the world's first artificial satellite.

The NSW Government decided in 1958 to run a lottery to help finance the cost of building the Opera House and the same year saw Uluru National Park declared. An automatic telephone exchange opened in Armidale. Equal pay for women teachers began in NSW.

The construction of the Opera House began in 1959 and 1960 saw for the first time in Australia the quantity of minerals exported surpass that of agricultural products.

Locally the UNE opened its Archives, employing an archivist and Ryans Cordials installed an updated plant.

The Parkes Telescope, the second largest in the world, opened in 1961 while in Sydney there were no more trams.

Perth held the Commonwealth Games in 1962 and Rod Laver became the first Australian tennis player to win the Grand Slam. Night landings of aircraft began in Armidale.

Queen Elizabeth II and Prince Philip undertook an extensive tour of Australia in 1962 and this year was the last of The Intermediate Certificate. The move to The Promised Land was completed not long after the Queen's visit and PLC Brown Street became an unpopulated area ready for the consideration of real estate agents.

Christine Prowse (née Heydon) 1957-1963

I was ten years old and a very shy country girl when I arrived at PLC in 1957.

I started in Prep House, run by Miss Hutton who didn't seem to like little girls very much. Despite the homesickness and spartan surroundings (three minute showers, saggy-based iron beds, chilblains from lack of heating) it was all very exciting, particularly night times in the dorm after lights out. We played pranks on each other and, to this day, I feel guilty for making Sue Gosper's nose bleed when I put sneezing powder in her bed. Sorry, Sue! I remember the thrill of being selected for the swimming team. I remember the fig tree outside Prep House (I wonder if it's still there) from which we surreptitiously stole treats on frosty mornings on our way to the swimming pool for early morning training.

The first person I met, Jane Daish, became my best friend in that first year and is still a good friend, 63 years later. She had long blonde plaits, a freckled nose and looked like Pippi Longstocking. Her plaits lasted all of two hours; her mother had to take her to the car and cut them off before she could start at school! We all had terrible pudding basin haircuts at that age.

My years in the school swimming team didn't last too long as asthma came in full force when the going got too exciting. One year I had to miss the inter-school swimming carnival as nervousness had landed me in sick-bay. After that I turned to netball, which was at least a warmer sport.

Living so far from Armidale meant that to get to school at the beginning of term, my sister and I caught the diesel train from Merah North to Werris Creek. In this hot, dusty little town there was a two hour wait for the train from Sydney, which arrived bursting with excited uniformed children bound for the five boarding schools in Armidale. I never did understand why parents sent their children so far when Sydney had plenty of good schools.

We had to be tough (manifested in shutting down) as there was no one to turn to in times of angst. There was no point in self-pity as there was no one to give the pity. I wonder if most boarding school children today would react the same way or if they have more pastoral care. We would have benefited from some of the philosophy of resilience taught in schools today. We just floundered/forged on, suppressed our feelings and pretended all was well. Maybe all was well.

Break times were filled with 50s-style games: cubby houses, jacks, skipping, cats' cradles, chase, ball games against a brick wall. It all seems very Victorian now.

The food was a joke/no joke! Sunday night was particularly bad; one boiled egg and one tomato rolling around on the plate! Our parents convinced themselves that we were well fed because most meals were all stodgy carbohydrates. Jamie Oliver would have had a fit. Like all boarding schools, we had our names for the dishes. The one I remember most is Murder on the Mountain for wobbly white blancmange with red jelly crystals sprinkled on top. It was repulsive.

The dining tables had a mixture of children from all classes, a good age mix. At lunch times, a member of staff sat at each table. We couldn't go for second helpings until our staff member had finished. We dreaded having Miss Cooper at our table. She was the very tall, very thin and very amenable Biology teacher who ate SO slowly that, if you had her at your table, you never got a second helping. We also dreaded our turn to sit at Top Table for the week to make conversation with the Head. She once asked me what I thought of the new Chanel suits. I had no idea what she was talking about! Where did she think we imprisoned children would hear about the world of fashion?

And imprisoned we were. No walking down the street, even in our final year, aged 16. By then the Head was Miss McLean who arrived in my class's final year and decided that we were a naughty bunch and should have all privileges rescinded. I'm not sure we were so naughty;

we just reacted against all the new rules imposed on the, till then, rather easy-going school.

Junior and Main House were an improvement on Prep House in terms of comfort. Mrs Vickery in Junior House actually seemed to like children. None of the houses had heating in the dorms….and Armidale winters were FREEZING. Only the classrooms had radiators and our pleated bottle-green tunics became flat and shiny from us taking turns at break times to sit atop the radiators. In the early mornings, we would wake to see the drips from the garden taps frozen into mini waterfalls and our lisle stockings on the clothesline frozen to the point of snapping in half if bent (maybe I imagined that bit)! Nor did the cold stop the early morning whole-school crocodile run around the block. How the neighbours must have hated being woken by the clamour of 120 girls thundering by like horses on the pavement! The cold was not allowed to stop normal life. On one freezing weekend we drove through thick snow and horizontal sleet over the mountain to Guyra to compete in a netball competition in our skimpy sports tunics. I've never been so cold in my life. On the way back in the car, we came across several cars which had side-slipped into ditches on the icy roads.

At some stage my year was housed a block or so from the main site in Brown Street. The excitement of actually walking outside the school confines was only exceeded by the thrill of passing TAS boys on the way. Boys were a total mystery, another species, forbidden, exciting. There were no male teachers in the school (apart from, briefly, a German teacher) so the opposite sex was only encountered in school holidays.

The freedom of day girls to come and go (and to have boyfriends) was envied but I'm sure they felt they were missing out on the dormitory shenanigans. These after-lights-out escapades really only amounted to whispering and giggling in the dark and the very occasional (not-so-midnight) feast. If caught, we stood for a while outside the Head's door, shivering on the bare floorboards in the unheated hallway.

I remember always hating pointless rules (and do to this day) and just had to kick against them. One example of a pointless rule was that hat brims had to be down at the front so I wore mine up, despite endless tickings-off. Despite the defiance, I liked lessons and particularly those of the no-nonsense but very stimulating English and History teacher, Mrs (Gwen) Kelly, who was a great intellect (and published author). The other memorable intellectual mind on the staff was the liberal and alternative-thinking head for four years from 1959, Miss Joan Humby, who was English. We were all terrified of her but she liked to see spirit and encouraged us to be unconventional and think out of the box. These two women were both nonconformist and inspired me. They tolerated my rebellious nature and, no doubt because of them, I went on to teach for many years in a progressive school in London, King Alfred School in Hampstead.

In my penultimate year at PLC, I was caught smoking (with Sue Kilgour, I think) in the sports shed. Miss Humby was definitely not impressed - which was a blow as I wanted this clever, unorthodox woman to rate me.

Gwen Kelly wrote, among other novels, *The Middle-Aged Maidens*, set in a girls' boarding school and very obviously the story of life at PLC. One incident in the book narrated a conflict I had with the new Headmistress, Miss McLean, in my final year in 1963, and therein lie two stories.

Miss Humby was much respected by the girls (we were scared of her razor-sharp mind) but apparently not by the governing board which reacted to rumours about one of Miss Humby's friends. Consequently, the board of the school in 1963 decided to act and, sadly, she was moved on, to be replaced by, Miss McLean, who seemed to think that the school needed purging of the Humby sympathisers. Strict new rules were introduced to which we prefects of the final year objected. The rules were tightened, all objections ignored and the prefects demoted to be replaced by six from the younger year. There was a massive outcry from our year and we stuck to our guns in protest until, I think urged by the reasonable Miss Cooper and Mrs Kelly, Miss McLean gave in and reinstated us.

However, it was war from then on. One of Miss McLean's rules was that it was forbidden to eat jam off a spoon. One day at breakfast she spied a younger child at my table doing just that. I was summoned, as head of table, to the Head's office and banished to sit alone at a separate table in the dining room for a fortnight as punishment for not 'controlling' my table. When my mother received a distressed phone call from me the next morning, she jumped in her car and drove 250 miles over dusty roads to the school, sat herself on the sofa in the Head's sitting room, refusing to leave until I was returned to my table. After hours at a standoff, both Miss Cooper and Mrs Kelly were finally instrumental, in the early hours of the morning, in persuading Miss McLean to give in to my very determined mother.

Lessons were traditional chalk-and-board and didactic in methodology but I always wanted to learn so I didn't mind. I even rather liked the adrenalin of exams. Parents didn't push children in those days, I don't think. Mine certainly didn't. They tended to leave education to the schools and didn't interfere. If we didn't work, that was our problem…and the school's. Having no life outside school meant we had plenty of time to study. There wasn't much else to do.

Sundays were spent sprawled around the grounds on rugs, reading and listening to the piano practice from the music rooms. We were allowed to open our tuck boxes from home, usually a biscuit tin, full of sugary treats. The favourite treat was a tin of condensed milk, twice pierced and then boiled until it turned to toffee. I have no recollection of where we boiled this confection but anyone with a tin was certainly popular. Sunday evening assembly in the Hall inevitably included the beautiful but dirgeful hymn 'Now the Day is Over', which always drew a tear.

All the little girls had crushes on someone in the final year. For me it was Anne Kermode. I wonder if she ever knew?

Hair was washed only once a week, on Saturdays. On one such morning in November 1963 I had my head in the basin in the Main House bathroom (why couldn't we wash our hair in the shower?) when we were told of Kennedy's assassination. A moment imprinted on the mind for life.

I can't remember what year we started to have dances with the boys from TAS, definitely the highlight of the year. I can still remember the shoes I wore to my first dance in the hall. Dancing consisted of the boring, but elegant, Waltz which we practised for weeks beforehand.

There is a sad tale attached to our class of '63. Margaret Lehman, who was very vivacious and funny, the life and soul of the class, married soon after leaving school. One evening in 1974, she was driving home from Tenterfield, went to sleep at the wheel of her car and died, leaving four young children under six. As I had already left Australia the year before, to live permanently in London, I have sadly lost touch with her husband and children.

The Brown Street site was not very spacious and so the annual prize-giving and Speech Day was held in a hall down in the town. The school in my day only had 120 pupils which meant small classes (sixteen in my year). I'm glad to see that the numbers are only 300 now in 2020. As a teacher, large schools and classes are anathema to me. Children need the intimacy of a small class to develop good relationships.

I think it was in 1963 that the school finally moved from the Brown Street site to the pristine new buildings on the hill, smart and modern but lacking the character of the Brown Street buildings. I think our year had one term up there before we left in December 1963. Only the dormitories were ready so we were bussed down every day to Brown Street for our lessons.

A wonderful new school, I'm sure, but I will always remember the Brown Street site as my PLC.

Jenny Johnson (née Burnett) 1955-1956

I followed my sister, Dinah Roepers (Burnett), to PLC for my 4th and 5th year only, in 1955/56. Dinah was three years ahead of me at PLC. I was in the then *Wentworth* sporting group and was housed in North Dorm in 1955, and East Dorm in 1956.

My previous school was Lismore High where I was very happy, so I don't think I would have been pleased about the change if we had not been moving to Sydney and change was inevitable.

I travelled to PLC from Sydney by train. Our travelling uniform was a smart bottle green suit which was occasionally mistaken for a Railway Hostess (they had them in those days) uniform, which always amused me. When I arrived (Tuesday 1st Feb) I do remember I was made very welcome. My diary notes: '2nd. Received text books. Played tennis in the afternoon. 3rd. Usual school. Played tennis in the afternoon. 4th. Swimming in the morning. Issued with stationery in afternoon. 5th. Sat in grounds and did prep. Blackberry picking in afternoon. Special tea for new girls given by 5th Year. 6th. Went to church and did prep.'

My diaries and leather writing case are still with me, though much worse for wear.

I also note that my brother, Michael, who had started his final year boarding at TAS, visited me that Sunday afternoon, as he did on numerous occasions during that year. The other thing I did that Sunday was write letters - also something I learned to do regularly at PLC and stays with me to this day, despite also enjoying the ability to communicate with digital technology!

When writing about sections of my life I am as much surprised by the things I don't remember as the things I do. I do remember having difficulty with study as there was no place to do this alone and undisturbed. Locking myself in a toilet cubicle resulted in people banging on the door insisting I leave! I have no recollection of staff names - except Miss McColl, our Headmistress at the time - but I do have images of others and recollections of events. Memories of an English woman who started a choir. She introduced me to singing in parts; I never sang soprano, always the lower part, which still to this day is the one I am most comfortable with. We sang Handel's 'Hallelujah' in two parts only, at our Presbyterian Church. My singing at PLC gave me the confidence to take up singing again in 1999 when my husband, David and I discovered Camp Creative which has been held in this mid north coast area (mostly Bellingen) for over 25 years.

We have a local *a cappella* group at Woolgoolga, but no singing in this 'Covid' year of course,

Moving house and situations seems to have always been part of my life, (on my fingers I am counting 18 houses in 11 towns/cities so far). Even at 17 years of age I was ready to move on, especially as Sydney living was quite different to Armidale or Lismore. Nevertheless, the in-school, and community experience gained at PLC, contributed to my ability to be able to make full use of my future and cope with its challenges. Our experiences were extensive, though I think the fact that I only arrived for the senior years may have allowed me to view and participate a little differently. For example, I had an older brother close to my age (2 ½ years between the three of us, with Michael in the middle); I had been attending mixed school classes, sports and dances since primary school; I was the youngest sibling so could feel some familiarity from their boarding experience.

Some of those in-school and community experiences were:-
- Had a go at all school sports, without too much prowess, but particularly enjoyed swimming (when warm!) and tennis. We visited most other Armidale schools and Teachers' College for sporting events.
- Missionaries and a local MP came to talk of their experiences, and make presentations.
- I participated in debating both in-school and with other schools.
- We watched at least one movie most weekends.

- We joined the Presbyterian Fellowship, attended meetings and church fetes.
- Ballroom dancing was taught in our own hall and we attended dances at TAS.
- Public events were attended, eg. Naval display; TAS Gilbert and Sullivan concerts; ABC concerts in the Town Hall; tennis tournament with Ken Rosewall and Mervyn Rose.
- We seemed to sometimes break school rules and boundaries without much ill effect, I am relieved to say!
- There were mid-term breaks (three terms only in those days). I occasionally stayed in but mostly spent these with local friends of our parents or good friends from school who kindly took me home with them.
- Excursions: We had a Biology Excursion to Point Lookout in September 1955. I remember because I took photos. A great day - not sure how much Biology we learnt.
- Attended the Armidale Agricultural Show.

Margaret Nowak (née Willis) 1954-1955

First Impressions: Coming as I did from a high school one of the first impressions was how small the classes were in what was then the senior years, 4th Year and 5th Year. There were 13 (or 14) in the year and not all planned to complete the Leaving Certificate exams. Biology was the only science subject offered and as I had not done this to third year (but Physics and Chemistry) my Dad talked the Headmistress into allowing me to do Chemistry which I did on my own with a UNE senior student as my teacher/ tutor. These days I marvel that the school agreed to that use of resources. There were two of us taking maths, general maths (with the Headmistress, Miss McColl), the only maths offered. As I remember three of us did French but the rest of the programme, English, History, Geography and Art had full classes of 13. Looking back on those subject choices is interesting; Biology or Botany was seen as the obvious choice of a science subject for girls and Maths at senior level was not encouraged. A stark contrast with the emphasis these days on encouraging girls into STEM subjects (Science, Technology, Engineering and Maths).

Another early memory is about food. In the first six weeks it was so good, really good. A real bonus was getting fresh baked cake or scones at morning tea, and hungry girls queued for that. Then came the let-down; for those first weeks, it seems, the cook was from UNE and when their students returned, our wonderful cook disappeared and it was downhill from there. Unrecognisable evening meals and no more morning tea cakes, only dry biscuits. I also remember being taken aside by one of the larger girls in my year and advised that if second helpings were on offer I should line up for that and this was then to be given to her. I tucked myself under the protective wing of one of the other girls in the year and then it did not happen.

My dorm was in Main House. I think there were about 12 of us in the dorm which would have been all the boarders in my year. Beds were lined up around the wall and we each had a small wardrobe with drawers, no dividers or curtains. Dorm life was fairly spartan but good; we shared much and it was never lonely. I remember there was a radio programme called *Inner Sanctum* which opened up with an ominously creaking door and had ghosts and other scary features. After lights-out, on whichever nights it broadcast, we would all listen to this, under the covers and ready to switch off at a moment's notice, and there would be little tremors and nervous giggles as we scared ourselves to bits. There were also opportunistic raids on the biscuit tin in the matron's office. I am sure it must have been recognised that these raids would happen and a blind eye turned.

For weekends we had a prep dress for general wear, sport uniform for around the tennis courts and a white dress with a big green bow at the neck, hats, stockings and gloves compulsory for going to church. Every Sunday the 'crocodile' of girls, two by two, would wend its way down and back about three blocks to the Presbyterian church for the morning service. A 'crocodile' would also often form for a walk on Saturday and the leaders would seek to direct it towards the boys' boarding school, TAS, for a glimpse of the boys. We were not free to go out of the school grounds on any other occasions (no trips to the shops) unless in the company of a prefect or parents, although there was one daring group who did sneak out to see the film *From Here to Eternity* (I think it was). There was much consternation and some penalty when this breaking bounds was discovered.

One of our favourite weekend activities was to gather at the tennis courts, of which I think there were four. We had rugs where we congregated on the edge of the courts and then when our turn came, had a game. My tennis skills became quite respectable. 'The Loft' was another place to congregate, upstairs from the gym and a small laboratory, a large open space where our suitcases etc were also stored but also space to congregate in gaggles and socialise.

The only local school we had any dealings with was TAS and that was rare. There was one school dance in my two years there, held in the dining room at Brown Street, on the occasion of a Newington College football visit to TAS. That created much excitement in the dressing up. Someone had a lipstick which we all shared; it may have been a day-girl because there would have been little place for having a lipstick at the school. I do not recall getting to watch the TAS/Newington football match which I guess was Rugby Union. The only other commerce with TAS boys that I remember was a couple of debates against them and I recall we did quite well there. I very much enjoyed being part of the debating team and suspect I enjoyed making a good point to confound the opposing team.

Girls in the senior years, largely restricted to 4th and 5th Years (equivalent of year 12 now), were taken on a few occasions to UNE, both for events there, such as investiture of a University Chancellor, and to visit the University Library. I look back on this now with gratitude as, coming from a small rural coastal town, I really had no prior concept of university and yet it was a post school destination which I was being encouraged by my teachers to consider. While this was a very oblique acquaintance with the concept of 'going to uni'. it, along with some teachers who were closely associated with UNE, was a support to me when I did make university my post-school destination.

The classroom: I was so very lucky with my classes at PLC. I had two teachers passionate about culture, in English and Art respectively, and two other teachers who took on a role as academic mentor and provided the type of learning climate which prepared me for subsequent success at university. Mrs Barrett was my English teacher; she was a passionate lover of Shakespeare and had LP records of some of the finest actors which she played in class. I well remember her playing the recording she had of *Othello* and how transfixed we all were with the drama of Desdemona's death and Othello's lament. Mrs Barrett had *Julius Caesar, Merchant of Venice, The Tempest,* and more besides. We loved it and as often as possible sought to divert class to this, rather than the dry study of essays or the set novel. For me it set-up a lifelong love of Shakespeare. Art was the other field where I found a lifelong passion. Miss Davies had a love of art history and guided us through the many developments in European Art, from Art which served the church to the more secular art of the twentieth century and all between. From her I learned about those artists, from Fra Lippi to Miro, which served me so well once I was lucky enough to travel in Europe and America, and fed a rewarding passion for me.

In my last year at school I had chosen to take History and Geography and study for honours in each. Gwen Kelly was my history teacher; she acted more as a guide and mentor and coached me in being a self-reliant learner. With her I was able to explore the UNE Library to support my study in Asian history for the honours programme and to expand learning into the full extent of the curriculum.

Lynette Lamberton was my Geography teacher. Two of us did the honours programme with Lynette, Hilary Weatherburn and myself. We were permitted to visit her home on Saturdays to work with her on Geography. Lynette's husband, Don, was an Economics lecturer at the university and he along with Gwen Kelly and Lynette encouraged us to consider university as a post-school destination. For me, in particular, this opened up new ideas. No-one in my family had studied at university, it was seen as probably unattainable and certainly an unlikely path for a girl. Thus my study in these two subjects at PLC, with the influence of Gwen Kelly and Lynette and her husband, set my life's course. I did apply to and got into Sydney University, I ended up studying Economics as Don Lamberton had encouraged me to do and my career path from there in economic research and university teaching was set.

I also credit Gwen Kelly and Lynette Lamberton in particular with opening up the opportunity to discuss broader questions around social equity. I do remember then, at home, getting into strong discussion with my Dad who did not quite go along with all the new ideas I was exploring, especially on attending university (though he was very proud in the upshot) and in views on equity and race. Having the opportunity to be mentored in a broader sense by these two strong and interesting women, because of the almost one-on-one work I necessarily did in my classes with them, has been a continuing influence on me.

Pamela Pike (née Golland) 1956-1958

I shared the prefects' dormitory with 5 other prefects in 1957. Judith O'Brien and I were new girls in 1956 and we became very close friends. We kept in touch following our school days until after I moved to Sydney with my husband and young family. Suddenly my mail to Judith was being returned to me and I had lost contact with her. Eventually in 2009 I discovered she was living in Cobar with her younger sister. My husband and I travelled to Cobar to see her. Judith was extremely ill, her big blue eyes the only recognisable feature from the bubbly girl I had known. She passed away in October 2010.

My daughter Alison also attended PLC Armidale in 1983 and 1984 while we were living in Sydney so we had many trips to Armidale during that time. The new school was certainly different to the old one in Brown Street.

A few things do stand out in my memory, like the terrible bathroom and laundry facilities. Who could forget the morning walks around the block crunching the ice under our feet in the winter time? The crocodile walks around Armidale on weekends were quite enjoyable. The food served in our dining room was mostly terrible, only saved by the large slices of fresh bread at tea time which caused me to gain a lot of weight.

If we wanted to have extra fruit it was permissible for our parents to arrange a weekly delivery from the fruit shop. I always looked forward to getting that.

I still remember the enthusiasm of Mrs Collins preparing us for the presentation of *Iolanthe* in 1956 when I was one of the peers.

My memories of coming back to Main House after prep each night are of Matron guarding the biscuit tin to ensure no one took a handful. She was an effective security guard also. I shall never forget the night she attacked a prowler outside our dormitory windows, shouting at him and bashing the hydrangeas with a hockey stick where he was hiding. He let out a howl and fled and I don't recall a reoccurrence of a prowler visit.

Catherine Gough (née McKechnie) 1954-57

So many memories. In 1954 Miss Davies was Acting Principal for two terms. Miss Jean McColl arrived 3rd term complete with pink hair and red rimmed glasses, driving a light blue (Mini Minor?) car; a very classy lady.

I was allocated to Prep House supervised by Miss Hudson. My room had two beds and was very basic. I was into sport, and coming from Moree and being blonde, all locals had green hair from the overuse of chlorine in the local public swimming pool. This was a bit of a shock to most of the pupils. I remember overhearing someone saying, 'Have you seen the new kid with green hair?' I was mortified.

My sister Toni and I were in *Forrest* House and were key movers in having *Forrest* for the first time in a long time placed 1st, a proud moment. Mum sent me a tennis racquet and I had lessons.

In 1955 I won the Junior Championship (athletics), was in the A Team of swimming, softball and basketball (netball). I should have applied myself more to my studies, but managed all subjects although could have done better. Oh *to put old heads on young shoulders!*

In 1956 I was transferred to Junior House. Miss Mears was in charge. We nicknamed her 'Dougan' after Dougan & Mears who were notorious escape artists in the criminal world. Later, after the death of our beloved nursing sister, Miss Mears took over the school hospital. I had an appendix attack and was sent by ambulance alone to Armidale Hospital. I remember crying all the way and the poor ambo trying to cheer me up. I was three days there under observation before returning to the school sickbay, appendix intact. In winter in Junior House we were rostered to collect vats of cocoa from the kitchen, skin all broken up in it. Yuck! I still dislike skin on hot milk.

A group of us decided to brighten our lives and 'break bounds' and go to the local shop to buy soft drinks and sweets. Not being completely stupid, we pooled our money and decided it was too risky for all of us to go, so we drew straws to see who did 'the shopping'. I was disappointed not to be a shopper but we all agreed if caught we would all own up as the guilty ones. Between Evening Prayers and Prep we ducked out and scoffed the ill-gotten gains; I don't remember enjoying it much.

Imagine our horror when at about 10.00 pm the whole school was woken up and marched to the Assembly Hall to have Miss McColl tell us that she knew girls had broken bounds and 'unless the guilty ones came forward all the school would be punished.' So forward in our dressing gowns we all stepped, BUT so did 5th Year girls and they were the ones seen down in the park talking to boys. We were the small fish caught up in the net and unlucky to have chosen that night to go shopping! This was the only time I was ever involved in any illegal carry on; I did naughty things but nothing to harm anyone and always owned up. Consequently I was never punished for 'naughtiness'. Our punishment for shopping was gated for mid-term, not allowed to watch the Saturday movie *The Cruel Sea*, and not allowed to participate in the Gymnastic Display of which I was a member. Terror was our parents were to be told; but it all fizzled out. I would have loved to know the thoughts of Miss McColl when we all stepped forward!

I detested the morning run but not as much as when, towards the end of 1st term, getting up at 6.00 am to walk to the Council pool to train for the inter-school Swimming Carnival. It was so cold, thinking of the warm bed I'd vacated.

Moree being too far to travel home for mid-term my friend Heather Noon always invited me to her home at Walcha Road. Heather (Bev) and I still talk at least once a month as I do with Beth (Hallam).

Not bad for 70 years! I'm also in touch with Jill Gunthorpe.

Once a year the school went on a picnic by bus to the Pine Forest, given two sausages to cook over an open fire, and eaten as 'sausages on sticks' or more like 'raw sausages with blackened outsides'.

My dentist was Mr McBean (Billy). He was on the School Board and used to swear so much. I had a fair few gold fillings installed and years later was always asked, 'Who did your dental work?' Scared me but he was good.

I moved to Main House where Miss Williams was our House Mistress and if we were caught talking after lights out she would make us sit in the hallway outside Miss McColl's room where we sat hoping Miss McColl would not open her door. To my knowledge she never did. I would love to read Miss McColl's recollections of her PLC tenure.

Every second Saturday we had a movie of Miss Davies' choice. Norman Wisdom seemed to be her favourite actor—boring! Occasionally we'd snag a good one. Other Saturdays we just had dances, girls only, but it was fun.

The Ides of March was supposedly the anniversary of when Lily Phillips was allegedly run over by a car on her way to a music lesson. For the new girls' benefit, on that date, we'd spread music sheets near their beds with blood on them pricked from our fingers—charming!

OH! THE FOOD. Always hungry. Sunday nights as a treat, left over cakes came from a local bakery. We would have to take it in turns to sit at Top Table with Miss McColl at lunch time, dreading that it would be stew with brown cabbage as we had to eat what we had been served. Breakfast with boiled eggs we'd always peel them and usually someone would say 'chicken!' Appetites gone!

At Lent most of us sacrificed something. I gave up milk in my tea, did not like black with sugar so gave up sugar. When Lent was over I could not go back to milk and sugar and to this day I have straight black tea and coffee. One girl gave up marmalade jam—she detested it.

We had eight to a table in the dining room overseen by a prefect. Going into breakfast our shoes were inspected to see if they were clean.

We were only allowed down town (dentist appointment etc) accompanied by a prefect. Coffee Inns were popular and totally banned. They had guitar players there. One prefect took me to a café to have waffles and ice cream, a famous favourite. I could not understand what the fuss was about and still do not like waffles and ice cream.

At the end of 1957, for some unknown reason, Miss McColl called me and another class mate to go down town and collect a record she'd ordered. Four years and this is the first time allowed down town without a prefect. Not to miss an opportunity, we made a quick call around for shopping lists. Off we went, collected the record and hit the shops. Walking back, 'BEEP! BEEP!' Oh No! Miss McColl pulled up. We scrambled into her car very uneasy and she ignored our shopping, WHAT A LADY! and thanked us for collecting her record.

I could talk longer about my experiences at PLC, like when Miss Williams, House Mistress at Main House, would go and pepper the roof of our dormitory with stones (remember a Girls' College was rife for prowlers) but one time someone saw her, so we all did the usual SCREAM and yell PROWLER! All a laugh.

In summary not much comfort, food really bad (and I'm not a fussy eater), really pleased to have been a boarder at PLC where I made lifelong friends.

Lorna Lewis (née Pitkin) 1953-1957

I am not aware how it came about that I went to PLC at all. I know I had dreams of wanting to be a school teacher and for that I had to go to High School first! I lived 26 miles away from a high school in South Grafton and there was no transport for me to be able to get there each day. I would have had to board with someone or attend a boarding school. My family had a cattle property at Kangaroo Creek and as I also had 3 sisters and 2 brothers it would mean we would all have to go away to school. It must have been hard on my family to send their children away at about 12 years of age. I had just turned 13 when I started my first year at PLC.

It could have been chosen with the help of the Presbyterian Minister but somehow I was booked into Presbyterian Ladies College at Armidale for my first year at High School in 1953. My mother took me to Armidale when I first started. From then on for each of the three terms I travelled to and from Armidale by bus. It was quite a culture shock for a bush kid to be at boarding school! I was very homesick at first and missed the freedom of the farm and my family. When winter came I felt the cold. Armidale is situated at quite high altitude in the New England Region of northern New South Wales and the winters were freezing. It sometimes snowed and the ground was often covered with frost when we went for our 'constitutional' walk/run in the morning before breakfast. The class rooms were heated with steam heaters but the dormitories were not.

The junior boarding house (Junior House) was the newest building and there were quite a few beds in each of the dormitories. The senior house (Main House) was once an old mansion and there I slept on an open verandah with only heavy wooden blinds to protect us from the weather. We had a dressing room and bathrooms inside the building but it was very cold on that verandah. I got chilblains every winter and they were very painful in the cold and very itchy when they warmed up during the day.

PLC was only a small boarding school with just over 100 boarders when I was there. It has since moved to what we used to call 'The Promised Land' in another location on the other side of Armidale. We were in Brown Street and the old school building has become a retirement village and nursing home. The first time I had a look over the very lovely new school and grounds was when I attended the 130th anniversary of the school in 2017. I was most impressed. It is now a much larger school with many more pupils.

Boarding school became the routine for me and my sisters. When holidays came we went home to Kangaroo Creek on the bus. We took our entire wardrobe and possessions home each holiday and it was a big production getting everything washed, cleaned and repacked ready for the next term. There was always a mid-term holiday, usually a long weekend, during each term. We were not able to go the 200 kilometres home for just a few days and so often we were invited to stay with friends who lived not too far away from Armidale. When we did this we had a chance to experience life on sheep properties. Sometimes we just stayed at the school and did nothing very much. We were not the only ones who stayed behind as some of the boarders came from long distances and even from overseas, or their parents were overseas. At the end of the year Mum would come up in the car to our 'Speech Day' and take us home afterwards. During the last two years I had my sisters, Valerie and Lucy at school at the same time as me. When they started at least they had some knowledge of what went on at boarding school. I was able to tell them of the highs and the lows of the life. I guess they also felt strange for a while and were homesick too.

Although I visited at term holidays I never lived at Kangaroo Creek again. It would have been a big financial strain on my family to pay the school fees for 6 children for five years! If the seasons were good and the cattle prices were high it would have helped. I was totally unaware of what was happening financially. Valerie started at PLC in 1954, a year after me and Lucy followed in 1957. Colleen started in 1960. I know that at the end of paying boarding school fees for us all, including my brothers, from 1953 to about 1967 my family had very little spare money and must have gone without lots of material things so we could have a good education

I would have loved to have piano lessons but that was not possible with all the others to follow. I was used as a guinea pig for all my childhood and I thought at the time I was 'hard done by'. However when I grew up I realised I had been in a privileged position in the family and I am sure having to assert myself and help in the house and with farm duties I was learning valuable lessons in life.

Apart from the occasional homesickness at first and when things went wrong, I really enjoyed being with lots of friends at boarding school. I played tennis, netball and softball and was reasonably average at those sports. I was even in the swimming team one year! This was all a bit of a joke as I was in the event called 'The Plunge'. It was probably for non-swimmers as the participants had to dive in and stay with face under water with only one breath for the longest time and distance. This took a considerable amount of courage as I had to make sure I was on the outside lane so I could paddle over to the side of the pool when I came up for air! I didn't really learn to swim until I was 16 years old and then I went with all the little children to 'Learn to swim' classes in Grafton during one summer holiday. This also took a lot of courage. I did learn but I have never been a confident swimmer.

Learning Latin for one year and French for three years to my Intermediate Certificate was not a great experience. I was not good at these subjects and was not interested at that time. I regret it now as I would have been much better at learning the European languages. With all the travelling I was to do later in life it did mean I had learned a lot of the roots of words that would help in translating other languages. I was no maths scholar either but managed to pass most of the time. I loved English, History, Geography and Biology though and these were the subjects I passed in my Leaving Certificate. I did pass my Leaving Certificate with a very ordinary pass at the end of my school years at PLC. I did not pass Maths or a language in my final year so I did not *'Matriculate'*. This meant I could be accepted for Teachers College but I could not go to university. I was not worried as I didn't work very hard until the last year and I achieved what I set out to do.

I did do my Leaving Certificate again while I was working at my first job as a library assistant at Grafton Library. I got a much better pass with 'A's but still no maths. That library was my first job and being a librarian was my last job. Before I retired I was a Library Technician in a Library in Melbourne. The rest is history.

Christine Perrott (née Ewing) 1953-1957

My family had moved from Sydney to Guyra in 1951 and I went to Guyra Central School in 1952. I was the eldest child and a decision had to be made about my secondary schooling because Guyra Central School offered classes only to the Intermediate Certificate, 3rd Year. Armidale, about 28 miles away down a very steep incline called 'The Pinch' had a number of Secondary Schools which went up to the Leaving Certificate, 5th Year.

As far as my mother was concerned Armidale High School was out of the question because the girls stayed in a hostel. She imagined poor supervision and ventures, or even adventures down the town. These could also involve boys. NEGS was approached but was booked out, St. Ursula's was the wrong church denomination so this left PLC which agreed to take me.

The uniform list was daunting especially as each garment had to have a sewn on label commercially embroidered with one's full name. There appeared to be a different dress for many occasions, and different tunics, blouses and hats for summer and winter, socks for summer and lyle stockings for winter. An expensive regulation blazer, suit and woollen overcoat was listed as required as was a regulation jumper. How many of each item to include was provided, even for socks and hankies.

I arrived at PLC full of excitement feeling so proud in my uniform only to discover I was wearing my panama hat incorrectly; the brim was turned up all the way round. Mortified I hung my head not brave enough to either look at anyone or alter the brim.

I started in Junior House in a dorm that was probably once a verandah of the cottage. Adjoining it were rooms with wardrobes and chests of drawers for our clothes; each of us designated one drawer and a bit of hanging space.

I remember little of this time not even the House Mistress's name. At the start of each term one would try to get to school in time to 'bags' a bed of choice. I think it made little difference; all were basic iron beds with wire under shelf, kapok mattress, not many blankets, lumpy pillows and a bedspread of questionable age.

I remember more of my time in Main House where I began in South Dorm, then North Dorm (an unenclosed verandah with roll-up blinds) and later in a Prefects' Dorm where were had more space and more room for our clothes. While in North Dorm I experienced snowflakes floating towards our double bunks which were against the far wall. To deal with the cold most girls brought eiderdowns and bed socks from home, as well as old copies of the broad sheet newspaper, the *Sydney Morning Herald* or sheets of brown paper to place under the mattress and between blankets. Some went to bed in many of their day clothes like jumpers as well as their pyjamas or nighties.

Miss Buchan was the Headmistress when I started; a New Zealander who gave the impression of knowing what she was doing. A number of improvements were introduced to make life more interesting and stimulating; films on some Saturday nights, attendance at ABC concerts, at NSW Arts Council plays and I think she was responsible for adding Eurhythmics (a type of group gymnastics to music) to the dull PE program. She encouraged school performances. These became a recurring feature after she left and I recall acting and singing in Gilbert and Sullivan's *Iolanthe* as Lord Mountararat who I jokingly called Lord Milk arrowroot. A few of the roles were sung by adults like the English teacher's husband, Mr Aubrey.

On Sunday nights the seniors could go into Miss Buchan's apartment in Main House in their black velvet dresses with lace collars to be read a novel in serial form. She however made no change to the heating in the boarding houses which did not exist. Only the classrooms had heating, inadequate but better than nothing, especially if you could sneak your damp smalls onto a heater to dry, illegally of course. Miss Buchan was lured back to NZ, leaving at the end of 1954.

Next we had Miss McColl who had these amazing red frame glasses and drove a cute car. To us she was glamour personified and a contrast to Miss Buchan who was short and dumpy.

The dormitory schedule was set and included 'lights out' times and no talking thereafter; hair, comb and brush wash on Saturday mornings, allocated shower times, often timed (3 mins) by a prefect; and laundry and bed linen put out and collected at certain times. Food was forbidden inside the boarding houses and, unless it was raining or sleeting, all morning and afternoon teas and weekend recreations had to be held outdoors. For morning and afternoon teas we had bread with some awful jam like melon and lemon and sometimes an apple. I used to eat all but the stem of my apple and learnt only later that apple pips have some form of poison in them.

Once a group of us planned a midnight feast. It was so exciting, just like the stories in English novels until we were sprung. Next day standing before Miss McColl she made a strange comment to me. I'd just recovered from a bilious attack, 'Christine', she remarked, 'all that acidic food after what you've just experienced.' I was mortified in being singled out and had no idea what she meant.

When I first arrived at PLC, we were told that meals were held in a new dining room with its own kitchen, changed from the Main House where the old dining room had become a dorm. The new dining room was an ugly building like a big farm shed. The meals were memorable for being less than acceptable and at times, like Sunday tea, meagre, requiring a fill up on bread and the spreads we were allowed to bring like peanut butter and vegemite. One breakfast I recall because of its strangeness. We were served stewed apples on toast. I think a new cook had arrived and his mastery of English was basic. The midday meal was the main one of the day and varied in acceptability. Many desserts were unbelievable like solid lemon sago/tapioca or sloppy bread and butter pudding. It was a relief to get jelly and ice cream or tinned peaches and custard.

Mid-terms were a welcome break usually involving going home or, if you didn't live close enough, going to a friend's home. I remember one of these I spent down near Walcha, a sheep grazing area. During the car drive down to my friend's sheep property the paddocks were littered with little white mounds which, to my horror, were dead new born lambs perished because of a cold snap.

Sports included tennis, netball, softball, swimming, athletics but strangely not hockey. Both athletics and swimming had annual carnivals and we'd cheer for those in our House to do well and get points so our House came first. There were four Houses, *Forrest, Macquarie, Wentworth*, and *Gregory*, all named for men. At least they were part of Australia's history.

Unlike bigger high schools, each senior year had a classroom and the teachers came to them unless the lesson required the gym, art in the loft, or science or sewing. I was interested in the academic lessons but also keen on sport and having fun with my friends. Many of my reports commented, 'intelligent, but lazy'. I hated Dressmaking classes and arranged to make my piano lesson clash with them. In my second year I went to the first sewing class. The teacher looked at me and said, 'Are you a new girl? What's your name ?'

The cold climate not only affected the dorms. Those of us in the swimming team walked to the local pool for training at 6.00 am. My piano practice was also scheduled for the early hours with just a one bar electric heater at 6.00 am. Even the run before breakfast was agony for many especially those whose homes were down the coast with its benign climate.

The school day began and ended with an Assembly which was a short religious service with a hymn or two. It included announcements and reminders. Sometimes it was my turn to play the hymn which made me very nervous. Less nerve wracking and even fun was playing the piano for our Saturday dances between us girls. I mostly played appropriate tunes by ear; waltzes, quick step, gypsy tap and the like.

I remember doing a forbidden activity in the science room where there were Bunsen burners and containers. I don't remember there being anyone with me, but I'd managed to get some onions and potatoes out of the store and took them to the science room, sliced them finely and cooked them in some butter saved from meals. It was delicious. I think we were often hungry and even at meals had to fill up on bread and spreads. A lot of us gained unhealthy weight.

The School Hospital with its live-in Sister always smelled of disinfectant. Cough medicine, aspirin, bandaids and bandages, Dencorub, cold and hot packs were distributed as required, scratches, grazes, cuts and sores bathed with Dettol and dabbed with iodine (bright yellow) or mercurochrome (bright pink), all with a dash of TLC. If necessary the doctor was called and the diagnosis might involve a few days in bed, or being sent home or going into the local hospital. I had a scare with a lump in my breast and, in tears went with my friend Anne to see Sister. She calmed me and called the doctor who said he'd come again next week and check but that he felt it was nothing to worry about and would go away. This it did, phew!

Another time I developed a sore and swollen foot and ankle from a small area of broken skin at the back of my foot caused about a week earlier by a long bench toppling and catching the back of my leg. Sister gave me a bucket of warm water with Dettol in it and told me to place my foot into it. To do this was unbelievably painful and she decided to pop me into one of the 'wards' for observation because I had a high temperature. As I lay in bed lots of strange creatures began to walk around on the walls and ceiling and I became frightened and called Sister. She realised I was hallucinating, saw the red line going up my leg and called the doctor. The upshot was I was sent home to be under the care of the local GP who came daily for a week and administered an antibiotic injection. I had developed cellulitis.

The outside world intruded little on our school life but I do recall the Armidale town march for the Coronation in June 1953 where we joined other schools and many organisations and businesses to walk down Beardy Street with flags and banners. Another world event which took my interest, I don't know why, was the Suez Canal crisis. In 1956 the Canal was nationalised by Nasser of Egypt thereby controlling a once freely used Canal for important shipping, particularly of oil. I seem to remember listening to news of the crisis on a transistor radio under the sheets after lights out. I can't remember the outcome!

One cool evening after dark we all went outside and stared at the sky to catch sight of Sputnik, the first artificial satellite which was launched in October 1957 by Russia. As we had no idea what to expect and had been told only that it would not twinkle like a star many of us missed seeing the tiny bright spot moving slowly across the sky. We had no inkling that this heralded the Space Age.

I remember we were cruel to a new teacher in 3rd Year telling her made up given names as she went around the class attempting to learn our names. Instead of giving up and making a joke like, 'Well I'm Cinderella and we'd better start the lesson' she ran out of the room in tears and never returned. Our teachers were a mixed lot and not all were university graduates or teacher trained. However those girls who wanted to do well enough in the Leaving Certificate to do further studies or training seemed to achieve their wishes. One advantage was the small classes because some girls left after the Intermediate Certificate (3rd Year). reducing class sizes to well under 20. A particular teacher favourite of mine was my music teacher Miss Adams. She was crazy about Bach and other composers of his era and I retain a love of early classical music.

Although for my Leaving Certificate I did English Honours with Mrs Aubrey and History Honours with Mrs Kelly, both university graduates, I attained only what was known as a gentleman's pass (how sexist is that!) of 5Bs. This was sufficient to matriculate into university but not enough for a Commonwealth Scholarship. I think the main problem was that I'd get incredibly nervous at exams, which in those years were the entire basis for the results. These nerves affected my handwriting which was not the best at any time and it became virtually illegible.

Without a scholarship it was too expensive for me to go to Sydney for my chosen degree, Social Work, so I went to UNE and did Arts with no idea of how I'd use it for a job.

Even here I couldn't take my choice of Zoology because at the end of 1957 the Science Block at UNE had burned down limiting the lecture and lab spaces and creating timetable clashes. Zoology clashed with English. I tried out a lecture in Geology but was left stone cold (ha!) by having to poke and prod little rocks to determine their hardness. In the end I chose Philosophy about which I knew nothing, yet it became my major and later was instrumental in my attaining a permanent lectureship at Armidale Teachers College.

I think my time at PLC influenced my lifelong abhorrence of snobbery and hubris. We PLC girls constantly drew contrasts between ourselves and NEGS girls whom we saw as priggish snobs. I don't know on what grounds we did so, except that NEGS girls almost to a tee, spoke with a plummy accent and looked at us with scorn. At shared dances with TAS they wore makeup and frocks far more glamorous and expensive than what we had and did not hide their feelings of superiority.

One feature of the *Birida* times of PLC was the encouragement to give everything a go and the development of the strengths and talents of each girl. There was no noticeable attempt to mould a 'product type'. Emphasis was placed on good manners, obedience and group support. What I know of today's PLC this is still so. In my case I had a go at everything and at my final Speech Day was awarded the Ferris Cup for all round ability. I think this cup is now awarded for something else.

Sally Cater (née Mills) 1948-1959

It has occurred to me just how many more fun and exciting experiences boarders must have got out of school than we day girls who were there for lessons only.

Most children attend more than one school. at least one for Primary and another for Secondary. PLC Armidale was the only school I ever attended, starting in First Class in 1948 and finishing in Fifth Year in 1959. During that time there were several Headmistresses, Miss Ashworth, Miss Buchan, Miss McColl, and Miss Humby. At one stage there was a period between Heads and Miss Cooper, who was Deputy Head, filled in for a few months.

I can't really contribute much to this book because I was a day girl, travelling each day on a bus that came from Uralla in the morning and back in the afternoon. One of the consequences of this was that I rather envied the boarders whose stories I would hear second and third hand about the fun they had after school hours.

In my early years the uniform consisted of a bottle green pleated tunic over a white shirt, which my mother always complained about ironing. The rules regarding the uniform were very strict. I was once reported to the Headmistress for being seen down the street in my uniform, but not in my gloves. Shoes had to be polished each day.

I only remember one school dance; we were allowed to invite a TAS boy and for those of us who didn't really know any, this was a dilemma. We were given names and I invited a name on a list. He actually turned out to be good company; I think he was as nervous as I was. When the boys arrived we had to meet our partner then take him to be introduced to the Headmistress, excruciating for both of us. The dance was in the building known as the Dining Hall. We did have fun despite the surveillance.

My most memorable year at PLC was my final year, Fifth Year in 1959. This was the only year that I became a boarder and was one of a class of 11 girls. Miss Humby was our new Headmistress who came to PLC from teaching at Frencham. She decided that we were now (almost) adults and arranged for us to meet in her living room one morning each week, before school started, to have morning coffee and a snack…and to chat in French! We loved it!

School life for people in my age group was quite different to the experience of children today. In Primary school we were expected to be quiet, to contribute only when asked. There wasn't much discussion on current issues, quite a lot of rote learning, opinions were rarely sought. This applied to all schools, not just PLC.

Jill Longworth (née Eames) 1956-1957

I attended PLC Armidale for the last two years of my high school education.

Having grown up on a farm east of Rylstone far away from any regular primary school, my primary education was undertaken entirely by correspondence. For the first three years of high school (1953-1955), I attended Mudgee High and was a boarder at the CWA hostel in Court Street, Mudgee.

I was booked into MLC Burwood (my mother's old school) for the last two years of High School (1956 and 1957) but some time towards the end of 1955, MLC informed my mother that the only place available for me was in the Business Studies program. We were not impressed with this information as it meant I would not matriculate and would be unable to pursue tertiary studies at university.

Therefore, Mum set out to find me another high school for Years 4 and 5. She wrote to many schools but most were booked out or didn't have the correct subjects. I wanted to do French, Chemistry, Biology, Modern History and English. Some form of Maths was compulsory. Finally, a place was found for me at PLC Armidale. The uniforms were purchased by mail order. I had to be outfitted in so many different pieces of uniform – tunics, shirts, blazer, jumpers, suit, sports uniform, after school uniforms, etc and every item had to have a name tag sown on to it; poor Mum!

Finally, the time came to set out for Armidale. Dad had become increasingly apprehensive about the long drive (590km) so we arranged to spend the first night at Kerrabee in the upper Hunter Valley with the Macdonalds (Mum's sister, Pix and her husband, Glenny). On the following day we arrived at PLC about 2:30 pm. In those days, PLC occupied buildings that were located a few blocks south of the main street of Armidale. I was extremely nervous and would have liked to have turned around and gone home. However, we were scheduled for an interview with the PLC Headmistress at 3.00 pm.

In the waiting area we met a couple whom my parents knew well, Enid (whose young brother was later to marry my older sister) and Ken Heydon. They were booking their two primary school aged daughters (Christine and Gwen) into PLC as well. As the Heydons had to drive back to their property at Wee Waa (about 250km away) that night, Dad gallantly volunteered to allow them to see the Headmistress ahead of us because my parents were planning to stay the night in Armidale.

At the interview the Headmistress said that Easter was only a 4-day break and I would have to stay at school because the travelling distance to my home was too great. I was very disappointed. Anyway we went to the dormitory which was called 'Sleepy Hollow'. It was a long dark room with 10 beds in it. I was in bed No. 9. I think Mum and Dad were a bit horrified at the sleeping accommodation but there was no turning back. So they left me and I was quite upset – so much so that Mum and Dad came back about 2 hours later to see if I was okay. I don't know what would have happened if I hadn't been okay!

So I settled into life at boarding school. It was different to Mudgee High School but I adapted quite well. I liked the subjects, especially Chemistry. Only three students were doing Chemistry for the Leaving Certificate. One, a day girl and the other, a boarder dropped out after a term, so I had the complete run of the Chemistry Lab. I had my own key and I would go there after school or whenever I felt like it. It was probably against workplace health and safety guidelines etc. but in those days no one seemed to care about such things.

There were several consequences of me having free access to the Chemistry Lab – one was that I got acid all over my school tunic. The acid was quite diluted so nothing happened until I sent the tunic to the school laundry and it came back with hundreds of small holes. Another problem was that I got silver nitrate on my hands and in the sunlight it turned black, so I had a black stain all over my hands for ages. Most importantly however, having open access to the Chemistry Lab probably led to my first job as a CSIRO Lab Technician.

Food at PLC was not too bad. It was repetitious and poorly cooked but edible. I didn't have the same access to shops as I had enjoyed at Mudgee, so I had to eat a lot more of the institutionally cooked food. On Friday nights we often had meat pies and tomato sauce. The same food was served for breakfast, dinner and tea on Saturdays. Sunday lunch was a roast dinner plus fruit salad and tinned cream. It was about the best meal of the week. During the week we took it in turns to sit at the top table with the Headmistress who would be observing our table manners and social skills. We had to remember to do the right thing and to eat everything. I seem to remember that we served ourselves from plates that were passed around.

I was a motivated student and enjoyed all the subjects except Maths which was taught by the Headmistress. She was a good teacher and we got on quite well – I just was not good at Maths. On the other hand, I was 'good' at English and History.

The day girls in our year came to the school on Saturday nights to watch the movie. Every Saturday night there was a picture show for the students. The movies were always in black and white and were usually a comedy to satisfy the wide student age range. There was always competition to see who would operate the projector. I never volunteered.

The first Easter at boarding school was a bit daunting because only four or five students stayed at the school. We were located in one building and could go down to the Armidale shops and buy food. I can remember buying a big jar of cauliflower pickles and eating that with some dry biscuits. Easter dragged by and on Monday the rest of the school students returned and school lessons started again on Tuesday.

The first holiday break for me occurred in May and I looked forward to going home very much. I caught the steam train from Armidale and travelled to Muswellbrook where I was met by Aunty Pix and Aunty Enid. Then we went to Kerrabee where I spent the night. In the morning we set out to meet Mum and Dad on the road between Kerrabee and Bylong.

Unfortunately, the drivers did not recognise each other immediately and both cars continued on in opposite directions. Once Uncle Glenny Macdonald realised what had happened he was very annoyed and said something derogatory about Dad. Anyway, Uncle Glenny turned around and chased after Dad. Then I was finally on my way home for my first holiday.

Like all holidays, my first holiday from boarding school went too quickly and before long I was back on the train at Muswellbrook going to Armidale. The train trips were quite enjoyable as there were lots of other students from other schools; Armidale was a mecca for education and there were five boarding schools located in the town at that time. There was also a dining car on the train which we made full use of because we knew it would be some time before those luxuries would be enjoyed again.

The local fruit shop in Armidale had an arrangement with PLC whereby they delivered fruit each week for individual girls. I received 4 shillings worth of fruit each week which in those days bought a lot of fruit. It came in a big brown paper bag from Aboods – I remember that 4 shillings was the highest amount spent on fruit and only two or three girls got this quantity of fruit each week.

When I first started to get the fruit I did not know where to store it. As I thought we were not supposed to have food in the dormitories I decided to put it in a cupboard used to store art materials and located in a loft in the grounds of PLC. To access the loft you had to go up some outside stairs and then there was a big room where art classes were conducted. This seemed like a convenient arrangement until the art teacher, Miss Davies, got up at a special assembly just before the evening meal one night and in a voice trembling with rage said that, 'some girl had had the audacity to store rotting fruit in the art cupboard.'

Then the directive was given that the fruit had to be removed or the person responsible would be reported to the Headmistress. I was really frightened of the consequences so I waited until the school had gone in for the evening meal before sneaking up the stairs to retrieve the fruit. I expected that Miss Davies would be waiting for me but she wasn't and nothing more was said about the matter.

In my second year at PLC we moved to another dormitory which was an open veranda on the ground floor with roll-up wooden blinds. The blinds had to be secured at night in case it rained. It was very cold but quite pleasant sleeping on this veranda. There were often vague sightings of prowlers and the police would be called to come and patrol the premises.

While I was at PLC we often tried to get sick so the school would be shut and we could go home. I think we had an outbreak of conjunctivitis and an Asian-flu epidemic, but the school wasn't closed. If you were sick you went to sick bay where an old, retired nursing matron dished out old fashioned remedies like 'gargle and swallow' or 'gargle and spit'.

Once, when I had a sore throat, I went to sick bay and was given sulphur tablets, told to go to my dormitory and go to bed. I followed these directions but after about 30 minutes I began to get very itchy – my tongue and lips became swollen and my eyes began to close. After a while I realised I was getting very ill so I got out of bed and made my way to the Headmistress's study. Her study was in the same building as my dormitory and fortunately she was there at the time. She called a doctor who came and gave me an injection and I recovered quite quickly.

Later, my parents received a letter saying that I had to see a specialist and be tested for allergies. So the next school holidays Mum and I went to Sydney where I was skin-tested for every conceivable irritant. I did not have a strong reaction to anything but a mild reaction to dust, peanuts and vegemite. I kept saying that it was the sulphur tablets but I still had to have the tests and Mum had to send the results to the school.

The second and last year at PLC went very quickly and before I knew it I was sitting for the trial Leaving Certificate examinations and then the real Leaving Certificate exams. Everyone in NSW taking any particular subject sat for the same paper on the same day. I had studied very hard and should have done well. Unfortunately, some of the questions that were on the papers concerned material that had not been covered by the PLC teachers. However, my results were not too bad. I got four Bs and one A. Furthermore, I was later able to upgrade my results to five Bs and one A. The A was in English but I had expected to get an A in Modern History as well.

While it was disappointing that some of us were not as well prepared by the teachers for the external Leaving Certificate examinations as we might have been, the school must have been doing something right because a day girl in my year scored the highest possible result in the Leaving Certificate and went on to achieve amazing results at university.

My experiences at PLC were mostly good. I learned a lot and met different people and teachers. We learned to be creative and inventive in occupying ourselves. I remember listening to the ABC on Sunday nights. We were allowed to listen to the Sunday night play and *Fire on the Snow* by Douglas Stewart made a lasting impression.

As is common these days, we also had a high school formal at the end of final year. However, it was a pretty tame affair by modern standards. Escorts were sourced from TAS. Most of us did not know any boys there but some girls had brothers or even boyfriends at TAS. We were all matched up, some more satisfactorily than others. Robin (my older sister) who was working in Sydney, got me a dress and I think it might still be at 'Eastwood' our old family farm where I grew up. Mum made me a red velvet top.

At the end of the school year Mum and Dad thought they might come up to Armidale to collect me. Dad had bought a new Chrysler Royal and this was to be the first time he had driven it on a long trip. There was some uncertainty hanging over the planned journey. Dad was concerned about leaving 'Eastwood' during the bushfire season but he was hoping for rain. They were also uncertain as to whether I would be getting a prize on Speech Day.

To encourage them to come I told them I was likely to get an award. In actual fact I only got the Bronze Medallion for Life Saving. In the end, Mum and Dad did make the trip and apart from attending Speech Day and collecting me, the new car was given a real test drive. After Speech Day was over, goodbyes were said, many promises were made to write etc. and we stayed the night in a hotel in Armidale. We left for home early the next morning and I think the journey was accomplished in one day. We probably visited Mum's sister and her husband at Kerrabee but I do not remember staying the night at Kerrabee.

The Christmas holidays passed quickly. The only excitement was the publishing of the Leaving Certificate results in the *Sydney Morning Herald*. Auntie Dot rang us early with my results which were OK. Dad said he was relieved that I had passed because he could not afford to send me back to PLC. I think that there was a drought on at that time. Anyway, it had never crossed my mind that I would be returning to PLC so I was surprised by his comment.

Thanks to my mother's persistence in finding a school that allowed me to take Biology and Chemistry (and my father for driving the long distance from Rylstone to Armidale), I think my years at PLC helped to build a platform which prepared me for a rewarding and happy life.

The subject choice at PLC (and the easy access to the Chemistry lab) allowed me to quickly pursue a career in laboratory work. Within months of leaving PLC, I was employed as a Laboratory Technician in the McMaster Labs of the CSIRO in Sydney. I was employed in this capacity by CSIRO for three years during which time I completed 2 years of the 3-year P/T TAFE Diploma in Laboratory Techniques. I completed the third and final year of this course while undertaking the first year of a degree at Sydney University.

In 1961, I enrolled in the BSc(Agr) in the Faculty of Agriculture at Sydney University and graduated with a Bachelor of Agriculture. This led to being awarded a NSW Department of Health scholarship to undertake a P/G Diploma in Nutrition and Dietetics.

Dietetics was a new profession and I entered it in its infancy. I was lucky to have many employment opportunities: Sydney Hospital where I was part of the team conducting the initial kidney transplants in Australia; an all African-American Hospital in Chicago; Royal North Shore Hospital in Sydney; and at different times at three of the major hospitals in Brisbane. I also attend an international Nutrition and Dietetics Conference in Kyoto, Japan.

I met my husband when we were undergraduates at Sydney University and we married while I was working as Dietitian-in-charge at Sydney Hospital. His work enabled us to live for extended periods in Chicago and in Kyoto, Japan (three times) and led to us settling in

Brisbane where we have raised five children all of whom are now married and living with their own families nearby.

When we were having our 5th child, I decided to take a degree in Social Work at the University of Queensland. My interest in Social Justice was awakened at PLC by the English and History teachers. After graduating in Social Work, I became a Cross-Cultural Counsellor at the South Bank Institute of TAFE. I worked mainly with refugees and other disadvantaged people for over 25 years in this role. It was very rewarding work and I still miss it.

In recent years, after being professionally employed for almost all of my post-school life, I am now enjoying a very full life as grandmother to five lovely families with a total of 14 grandchildren ranging in age from 21 years down to 18 months.

Jo Hawthorne (née McArthur) 1960-64

I spent three out of my five years at PLC being educated in Brown Street (as a day girl, when our family lived in a small part of D.D.H Drummond's large house in Mann Street) and the other two on the Promised Land where I was a boarder. I received a scholarship for my education, and when our family was planning to relocate to Sydney, the School Council approached my parents offering to pay my boarding fees to enable me to stay on at the school.

Miss Joan Humby was my Headmistress from 1960 to 1963 (I am not sure when Catherine McLean took over) and Miss McLean for my final year on The Hill in 1964. We had many teachers, the most renowned one was our history teacher, Gwen Kelly, and our tall German music teacher known as Sexy Sam!

When the boarding house known as McBean was opened in 1963, we slept there only, having all meals, classes and prep back at Brown Street; the journey up and down between the two sites being made by bus.

As day girls and boarders we played tennis, netball, softball and athletics at Brown Street, and went to the Armidale Swimming Pool for swimming lessons and our annual carnival there. Those who were taught music and were in the school choir enjoyed their time doing those things in the music rooms and the school hall, and occasional movies were screened in the latter.

TAS boys who passed by along Brown Street (or other streets nearby) were always of great interest to most girls during those days.

We had 2 sisters from Noumea, Nouvelle Caledonia, Michelle and Brigitte Danielle, attending as boarders for one year, and also two friends from Nauru, Daphne Amram and Margaret Jacob. I often wonder where they are now living.

I contributed to the 2017 Repast cookery book, and some comments I made about a few things can be seen in it on page 185.

In conclusion I can say that our mother (Gai McArthur being my sister) attended Hilton (on the corner of Brown and Dangar Streets) under the leadership of Miss Tendall as a 5-year old only child, and spent the last two years of her 92 in the Bupa Aged Care facility building, once the PLC classroom block where both her daughters were educated! Anything else I could say relates to PLC on the Hill, where I spent my last two educational years.

Best wishes to all PLC old girls living anywhere now…

Sally Robertson (née Price) 1961-1964

Miss Williams was the relieving House Mother in Junior House and we all thought she must be so ancient. She was doddery and repeated everything at least twice so was copied mercilessly. She expected me to be a good girl as she knew my parents.

On Sundays we all lined up to walk to church, in summer wearing our lovely white dresses with green pussy bows, the Presbyterians to St Paul's and the Anglicans to St Peter's Cathedral. A lot of us tried to be Anglican as they went to church at 9.00 am and then had the day free, especially if you had a Sunday Exeat (Leave Pass). St Paul's services started at 11.00 am and went for ages.

It was so good to be invited out by the day girls as even in the 1960s our parents thought it was too far to drive to see us even though mine were only 100 kilometres north.

Again the girls who had birthdays during the term often had parents come to take them out. There were also the Saturday morning phone calls and several girls had weekly calls but most of us rarely had them. However we did get our weekly letter from home with all the news. We were also expected to write home every week. How I wish we'd kept those letters. They would have been a mine of information.

Another memory is the morning and Sunday walks. Was it only Sunday or did we have to wear hat, gloves and blazer every day for those walks? The seniors led us and we always wished it would take us at least near TAS rather than the other direction. Of course, we were never allowed near the Main Street.

In 1961 I was in Junior House, West Dorm. East and West Dorms were mostly First Years but in West Dorm we had three Second Years. The dormitory prefects were Sue Ewing and Robyn Smith (Fourth Years) and Mrs Vickery was the Housemistress. Home Economics classes were held in the kitchen area on the south side of Junior House and the Rec. Room was quite close nearby.

Dorms had louvre windows so were cold in winter, hot in summer. Dark dressing rooms had drawers and hanging space allocated for each girl and tidiness inspections happened at random. That first year I got chilblains which I'd never had before even though I'd lived all my life just 60 miles north of Glencoe with a very similar climate. Some brought Teddies from home. Several First Years left after one year. Financial stress was the most likely reason, as mostly we all got on well and included everyone. Bathroom facilities were ancient.

The dining room was close to Main House. We knew which day of the week it was from the meals; Sunday and Wednesday roasts; Thursday corned meat (Mrs Johnson's day off). Memorable was the Apple Crumble topping which was quite hard, not crumbly at all. I was one of the few who lost weight during Term One as I was not a bread eater; how could you make that one small square of butter do more than one slice anyway? I do remember some girls (who shall remain nameless) flicked said butter squares onto the low ceiling, the grease spots being evident. Tables were mixed Years with a Fifth Year as head of the table. We'd line up at the kitchen window to get the food. We were rostered for sitting at Top Table for lunch with the Headmistress, generally once a term.

I remember the after lunch line-up out the back where Mrs Johnson would throw your piece of fruit (mostly apples or oranges) for you to catch. With those chilblains on the back of my heels they were often kicked by accident by the girl behind me. Ouch! I also remember being able to have a weekly order of fruit delivered from Aboods, paid for by our parents of course.

Tuck boxes were still allowed (later disallowed by Headmistress McLean/Hitler/Toothpaste) so we'd all come back with homemade cakes, biscuits, lollies and fruit. I SOOO envied girls who had a birthday during term as they could have more goodies sent for their birthdays! We mostly shared but I was very good at having just one or two pieces of chocolate each day to eke it out as long as possible. Some of my friends were envious I could do this and annoyed I kept something for myself.

Informal dances in the Rec. Room for the boarders (no boys of course) alternated with the movies Miss Davies screened on Saturday nights. Miss Davies also got a couple of cartoon films as well as a feature film and I hated Mr Magoo. I am very short-sighted, had thick glasses; it was all too close to me.

Come 1962 and I moved to South Dorm, Main House. Cold is the main memory again. No doonas, duvets or such back then to bring from home! I so envied the girls in North Dorm where they got glorious winter sunshine although they were closer to the Headmistress's quarters and her slobbering bull dog, Valli!

I think it was mid '62 when we moved to the Promised Land dormitories. What luxury with heating in winter and lovely windows on the northern side. Edwards Coaches provided the buses up at night and back in the mornings to Brown Street. We always hoped it was Junior driving just because he was younger and better looking.

Sport played a large role in our lives and choir for those the teacher deemed good enough to be in her choir. There was evidence of smoking up at the tennis courts.

Oh, and I do recall we had tuck shop in the tennis shed once a week and could get a bag of mixed lollies. I also remember the Guild marching practice around the tennis courts before the annual sports carnival.

I remember cold winter weekends where we would put tins of condensed milk on the heaters to warm up but if you were patient it would caramelise. Yum! Miss McLean was the Headmistress when I was in Fourth Year and she told some of us that there was no point in us going on to Fifth Year and attempting the Leaving Certificate. Some of us went to Armidale High School and passed the Leaving after all.

Mostly my memories are happy ones and great friendships were forged, but it did seem a long way from home.

Marlene Pearce (née Dew) 1960-1963

What fun and a great idea to have a book about the good old days at Brown Street PLC.

I was never in *Birida* (Main House) as I went straight from Prep House to the Promised Land and into McBean House. I was the first person to open the door with some other excited girls.

I do have lots of fond memories of my time at PLC although I left at the end of 3rd Year. My father was not impressed with my exploits and felt I was never going to achieve a Leaving pass and hence a career and he felt the school was at a low ebb.

Members of Junior House, 1956 - L-R Margaret Atkinson, Edith Lawrie, Valerie Pitkin, Liz Mitchell, Nancy Price, Jill Mitchell, Margaret Hutchison, Barbara Haun, Lillian Lawrie, Diana Lindsay, Catherine McKechnie. *Photo: Catherine Gough (née McKechnie).*

1957 Swimming Team. Back L-R: Ilsa Brunswick, Trudi Rodgers, Jill Fenwick, Di Turner, Lorna Pitkin.
Front L-R: Catherine McKechnie, Jennifer Burnett, Irmgard Brunswick, Helen Kiernan. *Photo: Catherine Gough (née McKechnie)*

1957 School with Headmistress, Miss Jean McColl.
Photo: Catherine Gough (née McKechnie).

1956 Prefects with Headmistress. Standing L-R Jennifer Burnett, Patricia Harrison, Caroline Muir, Sandra Noss, Sandra Black, Helen Muir. Front L-R Miss J McColl, (Headmistress), Irmgard Brunswick, Head Prefect.
Photo: Barbara McHattan (née Reid).

1954 photo of Miss Jean McColl, Headmistress. *Photo: PLC Archives.*

Dragoons in Gilbert and Sullivan's *Patience*, July 1957.
Photo: Barbara McHattan (née Reid).

Fourth Year Play, November 1957
Standing L-R: J Edward, M. Atkinson, J. Fenwick, R. Noble
Sitting L-R: J Roach, C. Burgess, V. Pitkin, N. McInnes, M Hutchison, J. Cassidy, H. Kiernan, J. Burnett. *Photo: Barbara McHattan (née Reid).*

Jenny Burnett and friend at the Agricultural Show
Photo: Jenny Johnson (née Burnett).

Tennis team, 1957 – Back: H. Fraser - Front L-R: B. Hallam, P. Jolly, C. McKechnie. *Photo: Catherine Gough (née McKechnie).*

Eurythmics display, 1958. *Photo: PLC Archives.*

Miss Cooper, Science Mistress and sometime Deputy Headmistress.
Photo: PLC Archives.

1957 Captains of the Houses (now called Guilds) Front to Back: June Wangmann, *Wentworth*; Christine Ewing, *Forrest*; Robyn Easterman, *Gregory*; Jenny Stephenson, *Macquarie*.
Photo: PLC Archives.

1957 Prefects, Head Prefect and Headmistress. L-R: Janet Navin, Robyn Easterman, June Priestley, Christine Ewing, Pamela Gollan, Judith O'Brien - Front: June Wangmann Head Prefect, Miss Jean McColl, (Headmistress). *Photo: Christine Perrott (née Ewing).*

Margaret Atkinson, Robyn Marks, Edith Lawrie and June Burnell trying to stay warm behind the tuck shop. We were not allowed inside at the weekends unless it was raining no matter how cold it was. *Photo: Beth McGee.*

Readying for the evening meal, West Dorm, Junior House. *Photo: PLC Archives.*

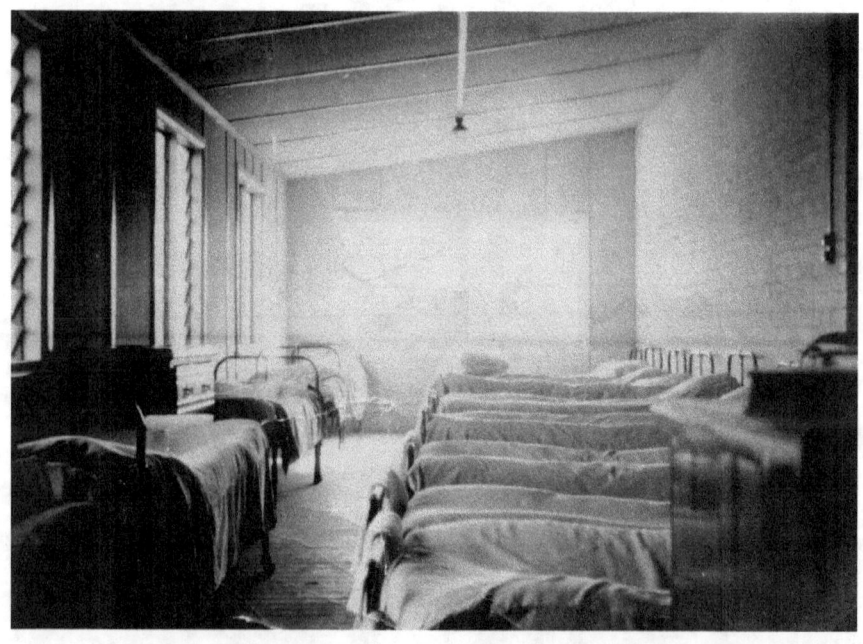

All tidy again, West Dorm, Junior House. *Photo: PLC Archives.*

Epilogue

So we come to the end of the recollections of some of the Armidale PLC Old Girls who attended the school in its Brown Street days. This group is now affectionately called 'The Birida Bunch' because their Main House in Brown Street was the elegant Federation home, *Birida*.

The reader cannot help but be struck by how little the routines, experiences and rules at the school changed over the period of the twenty plus years described. In the late 1950s girls were still hair washing on Saturday mornings, running around the block before breakfast and taking timed showers before the evening meal, followed by prep, wearing a uniform dress rather than the pleated tunic.

The uniform requirements make one wonder how parents were able to afford setting up their daughter for boarding school; summer and winter tunics, jumper, blazer and woollen coat (all green), suit (green), sports tunic (green) with tassel belt (blue), different dresses for church (white), evening events like dances and concerts (black velvet), for prep and weekends (green), going down town and out for weekends (blue). In addition there were white blouses (long and short sleeves), brown shoes, white socks, lyle stockings, black court shoes, tennis shoes, a panama hat, a velour hat and a regulation tie.

Another glaring factor is the conditions the girls lived under, particularly in the dormitories; no heating, with bath towels hanging at the ends of their beds frozen on the winter mornings, verandah dorms open to the elements and curious 'prowlers'. These would not be tolerated today, but most boarding schools at the time were similar in their expectations. It was usual for things like lumpy sagging mattresses, just one drawer and ¼ of a wardrobe's hanging space for each pupil, beds cheek by jowl and 'snacks' of stale bread with melon and lemon jam, were acceptable and not to be complained about.

The post-school achievements and activities mentioned in these memories, including Mayor of a rural city, a triple certificated nurse, a concert pianist, a novelist and a church minister, are testament to the school's culture which encouraged development of each girl's strengths, avoided trying to mould a certain type of young woman and discouraged sassiness and arrogance.

As bracing as the winter air is in Armidale I don't think *it* was responsible for providing the grounding for these successes. Peeling potatoes and playing the piano for Assembly hymns encouraged the importance of contributing, as did arranging and putting on plays and competitions between Houses. Supervising prep or trips to the dentist enhanced responsibility. No doubt grit was developed by having to deal with the cold, the before breakfast runs and unpleasant meals.

Shining out of these reminisces is an abiding love for PLC Armidale and gratitude for the friendships made there. This alone is testament to the success of the school before its move to the 'Promised Land', so long awaited.

Headmistresses of Hilton & PLC Armidale 1909-1968

Miss Alethea Tendall	1909-1938
Dr Helen Wilkie	1939-1941
Miss Clarice Ashworth	1942-1951
Miss Kathleen Buchan	1952-1953
Miss Jean McColl	1954-1958
Miss Joan Humby	1959-1962
Miss Catherine McLean	1963-1968

Acknowledgements

My heartfelt thanks to those who sent me submissions of their memories of school life when PLC Armidale was at the Brown Street site. Their honesty and obvious love of their time there despite many discomforts shines through. Some submissions were posted and handwritten, others typed, while many came as attachments to emails.

I owe gratitude to the PLC Old Girls Union for their encouragement, in particular to Kathie Marquardt who opened the PLC Archives for me and helped locate relevant materials, especially photographs. She also ploughed through the manuscript searching for errors and provided helpful advice.

The New England Writers' Centre, Paul in particular, was of great assistance in finding me the formatting, photo scanning and editing help I required.

Ian Hooper, Executive Director of Leschenault Press and their *Book Reality Experience* imprint, has been amazingly patient, providing clear answers to my often naive and ignorant queries. Thanks to him and his Press this book became, just as the title of his organisation suggests, a reality.

Thank you to the current Principal of PLC Armidale, Nicola Taylor. She marshalled her office troops to prepare and send mail or email to the relevant Old Girls requesting they send their memories for a proposed book about life at PLC Armidale before the move to the 'Promised Land'.

And finally, to my friend Helen Nancarrow, who kept me sane by offering an open ear and mind to my oft occurring panics and attempts to pick her brains about next moves. Helen even helped with proof reading. Thank you.

About the Editor

Christine Perrott has lived in the Northern Tablelands of NSW since the age of 11 and started at PLC Armidale as a boarder in 1953.

After the Leaving Certificate she did an Arts degree at UNE after which she had her first job as the Graduate Assistant at External Studies, the administrative arm of UNE's distance education provision.

After marrying a sheep grazier and producing two sons she returned to study and undertook a Dip.Ed. in Infants Teaching. She never became an infants' teacher as planned but was head-hunted by Armidale Teachers College (ATC) and began a career there, starting as an Assistant Lecturer. Twenty-five years and two post graduate degrees (MEd.(Hons) and a PhD) later, she finished as a Senior Lecturer in the Faculty of Education, UNE which had amalgamated with ATC.

She has written two books, *Classroom Talk and Pupil Learning*, HBJ and *Patient Fortitude*, Sid Harta. As part of her job she had many articles published in academic journals, gave many addresses and workshops at conferences, and in her retirement edited newsletters for various organisations.

She is an enthusiastic fisher having tried her luck as far north as the Tiwi Islands, knits garments with complicated patterns, loves doing her daily cryptic crossword, reading novels, attending classical music concerts, gardening, watching movies, writing letters to the Editor of *The Sydney Morning Herald*, travelling overseas, and catching up with friends. With four grown up grandchildren she also enjoys family get-togethers.

Much of her time is given as a volunteer to community organisations such as Helping Children and Families, she is a member of the Management Committee of the North and Northwest Community Legal Service, Vice President of Friends of Armidale Teachers College and still mentors and tutors post graduate students as well as recent Ezidi refugee arrivals to Armidale.

COVID-19 curtailed most of these enjoyments and she looks forward to receiving the vaccination and resuming loved activities.

Publisher's Comment

This fascinating collection of memories from the Old Girls of Presbyterian Ladies College, Armidale, is a snapshot of a time, not too distant in years, yet a quantum leap from the standards of education, accommodation, nourishment and pastoral care enjoyed by the current pupils of the many boarding schools within Australia.

This 'time-capsule' should be read as such and above all, one hopes the central takeaway is that despite the conditions, which we may view as austere and even stringent, the past pupils have reflected on the tremendous benefits they were endowed with by their time at the school.

They and the generations that came after them were the recipients of an education that granted not just knowledge, but resilience, confidence, fortitude and most importantly of all, lifelong friendships.

Yes they did indeed survive, but more than that, they thrived and we are happy for them to be able to share their stories.

www.ingramcontent.com/pod-product-compliance
Lightning Source LLC
Chambersburg PA
CBHW072008290426
44109CB00018B/2168